Black Girl Cry

**WHAT BLACK WOMEN NEED TO
KNOW TO AMPLIFY THEIR VOICES**

HEIDI LEWIS

publish
y⊕ur gift

BLACK GIRL CRY
Copyright © 2021 Heidi Lewis
All rights reserved.

Published by Publish Your Gift®
An imprint of Purposely Created Publishing Group, LLC

Printed in the United States of America

ISBN: 978-1-64484-481-6 (print)
ISBN: 978-1-64484-353-6 (ebook)

Special discounts are available on bulk quantity purchases by book clubs, associations and special interest groups. For details email: sales@publishyourgift.com or call (888) 949-6228.
For information log on to www.PublishYourGift.com

This book is dedicated to

my grandmother, Mary Louise Noel,

who taught me to dream bigger and see further.

Table of Contents

Acknowledgments

Councilor Mejia, you set the tone for this book.

Thank you to the Pentimenti Women's Writers Group. This tribe of women has pushed me to explore bold topics and new forms of expression. Special thanks to Ann Murphy, who proofread and offered feedback until the very last second!

Cheryl Polote-Williamson, you encouraged me to move forward with this project when some said it couldn't be done. I love and appreciate you.

Leisa Greene, thank you for believing in this project. Your kindness means more than I can express!

James Hills, thank you for Java and the introduction. I appreciate you.

Foreword

JULIA MEJIA, FIRST AFRO-LATINA
ELECTED TO THE BOSTON CITY COUNCIL

"Feisty."

If you're a woman of color in public service, odds are you have been introduced to a group of well-meaning white folk using that word. It's happened to me more times than I can count. And if it isn't "feisty," it's another word like "fiery" or "spicy" or any other word that makes me feel more like a Taco Bell menu item than an Afro-Latina City Councilor.

Why do people do this? It's because people of color, particularly Black and Brown women, are always expected to just occupy space in order to make other people look good. You'll hire us as your "Diversity, Equity, and Inclusion Manager," but you don't want to create space for people of color in your company. You want us to hold signs for your election campaign but you never want to listen to us once you get into office. You'll buy some smudging sage at the Dollar Tree, but you don't want to invest the time and money to learn about cultures different from your own.

It is this tension of expectations-versus-reality that leads to strong, vocal Black and Brown women being labeled as "feisty" or even "angry." Yet despite this adversity, women of color have been pushing through these concrete ceilings, and most importantly, dismantling the hurdles put in place for us so that the next generation can thrive. It's the story of every woman in this book, and it's my story, too.

As a woman of color, my professional career was halted before it even had a chance to begin. I dropped out of high school and got a job cleaning offices with my mom. I was almost 20 years old by the time I became the first person in my family to graduate high school and college. My mother was an undocumented immigrant who never got an education past the third grade and who, to this day, is still too poor to retire. In those days, when I would look over at my mother, I had resigned myself to thinking I would be cleaning offices for the rest of my life.

It wasn't until I had the opportunity to listen to Reverend Liz Walker speak that I realized that women who looked like me can do something more. Walker became the first Black woman news anchor in Massachusetts, and when I heard her speak, it's as if a light went off in my head telling me what to do. I went on to graduate high school and earn my degree in Communications from Mt. Ida College, being the first in my family to do so.

Years later, I managed to secure a dream job at MTV working as a correspondent for their *Choose or Lose* series. It was one of the first times I had worked with people from outside my own community, and I started to feel the tension between what was expected of me and what I ultimately wanted to do. I remember covering the 2000 Presidential election in Harlem. A group of diverse faces was standing outside chanting "Harlem wants Gore! Harlem wants Gore!" I asked the closest person to me, who happened to be a woman of color, whether she lived in Harlem. She gave me a look like she knew I had just caught her in a lie.

"No, I don't," she responded.

"Okay, so then who lives in Harlem here?" I questioned the audience. "Can anybody raise their hand and tell me who lives in Harlem? Harlem *wants* Gore, right?" I didn't manage to find one person in that crowd who actually lived in Harlem. It was in that moment that I was able to capture in real time how Black and Brown women are used as props to make a movement feel more authentic and more inclusive than it really is. The sad part is that there are actually a lot of people in Harlem who really *do* want to talk about politics and who *do* want to play a bigger role in their community, but they are just never listened to. "There are a lot of people in Harlem, right?" I told the group. "Why weren't we able to get *one* person who lives here to hold up a sign?"

I saw that perception of women of color all throughout my career, including during my time on the campaign trail and once we were elected into office. I was one of two Latina candidates running that year, and we were always lumped together. It wasn't because of our ideas, but because we both filled a role as a representative of a certain community. We both had to continually remind people that yes, you could in fact vote for both of us. It was as if the idea of voting two Latinas into office was as unnecessary as owning two pairs of the same shoes. To this day, people use the fact that I won my seat by a margin of one vote to suggest how fragile my position as the first Afro-Latina City Councilor is, even though 22,492 other people decided that our movement was worth their vote.

Since getting into office, we have worked to dismantle the barriers that were put in place for people like us so that more and more women of color can thrive—not just survive—in Boston. We rewrote the City's language access laws so that people of all different languages and backgrounds can be part of the process. We fought for a paid youth position on our City's Civilian Review Board so that over-criminalized young people of color have a voice standing up for them and their lived experiences. We passed a law that allows people to cook and prepare food in their home for retail profit. This brings local, culturally competent foods to neighborhoods that often lack good food access. We even started a Political Lab so that we can train people of color on how to run for office and how to run a campaign, something that no other agency or organization in the City is doing right now. We are putting power in the hands of the people because we know that nothing about us, without us, is for us.

Don't get me wrong, I still get looks when I answer a question in Spanish during a public hearing, or when I ask a well-thought-out question that they wouldn't expect "someone like me" to ask, but every day, more and more women of color are being put in positions of power to change that narrative.

So, to the strong women of color who read this book, let me say this to you: I hope that my words and the words of the other authors inspire you the same way Reverend Walker's words inspired me. In our society, we are still playing a game with rules we didn't make up, but this collection of stories is the playbook that nobody wants us to have. Use it wisely and never stop breaking those concrete ceilings.

Introduction

T here I was, standing in the entrance of the concierge lounge at the Grand Hyatt Hotel in New York. Me! The girl from the projects who made good. I was excited. I'd never stayed in a luxury hotel, let alone on an exclusive floor. I was in New York to speak at a national conference. I had been chosen by the leadership of the bank where I worked to talk about a cutting-edge product we were implementing. I had spent weeks working on my presentation. I was ready. Not only was I ready to speak, but I made sure I looked the part. I chose my sage Ann Klein suit and black patent leather slingbacks. So, there I was with the *Wall Street Journal* tucked under my arm and the briefcase my mom had given me as a Christmas gift. I scanned the room for a seat. All of a sudden, a white man walked up to me thrusting his dirty dishes toward me and asked, "Where do I put these?" I bristled. I'm sure my face flushed. When he realized his mistake (I'm using this term lightly), he said, "Oh, I'm sorry" and backed away.

I saw an empty table and rushed over to it. I sat in the seat, pulled the *Wall Street Journal* from under my arm and opened it so that it hid my face. I had to hide the tears that were pooling in my eyes. I didn't have to wonder why that man assumed I was the help. He saw a Black woman, and based on his own biases, assumed that I was. What he failed to realize was that "the help" were all white and had on navy blue uniforms. I remember sitting at the table blinking back tears, telling myself, "Don't you dare cry. Don't you ever let them see you sweat." The first time I wrote this, I realized that I had buried the pain of this experience. The tears came, hot and unchecked. I know I am not alone. There are other Black women and women of color who have also experienced the same blatant racism that has made them feel invisible. I also know that we are standing on the shoulders of women that have gone before us and paved the way. Women like Shirley Chisolm, the first Black woman elected to the United States Congress and the first Black major party candidate to run for President. Madame CJ Walker, the first female self-made millionaire; Katherine Johnson, the first Black woman to work as a NASA scientist; Misty Copeland, the first Black female Principal Dancer with the prestigious American Ballet Theatre; Michelle Obama, the first Black woman to serve as First Lady of the United States; Amanda Gorman, the first Black woman chosen as National Youth Poet Laureate; and so many others. While our grandmothers, mothers and aunts may not be famous, we are standing on their shoulders as well. As you read the stories in this book, be encouraged that you are not alone. You have a sisterhood that is creating a space for you to live your truth. I leave you with this poem entitled "Legacy." Think of it every time you get tired and the tears flow.

Legacy

I came in the backdoor so that you could come in the front.

I endured the beatings and the scars so that you could stand in my legacy.

I scrubbed floors on my hands and knees so that you could stand in the places I knelt.

My body was violated, my dignity stripped so that you could stand proud.

My voice was silenced, my purpose was taken, vision blinded so that you could speak in the mountain tops, vision clear, declaring who you are. Your destiny changing the earth.

My legacy, I saw you down the road. So I endured for you! Be brave, be fierce, be great. Step into the purpose predestined for you.

Living While Doubly Conscious

AYAH HARPER

I have always been good at shape-shifting. I am not talking about some superpower that allows me to turn myself into a coat rack or anything, but more so the ability to mold myself into whatever seems to be most compatible with, and convenient for, the people and environment around me. I never tried or even wanted to be able to do this, but in the past 18 years, it has become a habit that I cannot seem to break.

I went to a large, suburban private school from kindergarten through second grade. This is where I got my first experience with being the only shiny-faced little Black girl in a sea of green-blue eyes, brown pony tails, and pomegranate-stained cheeks. Early on, I realized that I had a knack for recognizing and remembering words. My dad and I would spend our 30-minute morning commute playing word games with the road signs, and I would come to school repeating the correct spellings of the new words I had just learned to everyone in my class. Before I knew it, students were lining up at my desk requesting spell-checks and word definitions, asking for help to come up with creative vocab sentences, and seeking solutions to any other language-related issue while the teacher had their hands full. I was honestly glad to do it; it made me feel wanted, necessary to the fabric of the classroom, and even a little bit special. It wasn't until things started to interfere with my recess time that I had my first "is this happening because I'm Black?" moment. The girls in my grade saw me swinging across the monkey bars and dismounting off the moving tire swing and insisted I teach them how to do it. Next thing I knew, I was spending what was supposed to be a break from my demands in the classroom teaching a bunch of amateurs how to replicate skills I had learned through my two years of competitive gymnastics lessons. It didn't take long before feeling "wanted" began to feel more like being employed, and I started to feel just as out of place as I looked. One day, after everyone else had gone out for recess, I confronted one of my assistant teachers about my dilemma. I purposely chose to leave race out of the conversation, asking her if she thought kids only sat at my table or wanted to be friends with me because they knew I had something I could offer them. She smiled gently, lowered her head to my level, and kindly suggested I move to another table in the corner of the classroom with only one seat so no one could sit near me. It sounded like a punishment—like a nicer way of saying, "If you don't like it here, then you can leave." I looked back at her sort of surprised and sad and helpless all in one. She was the first Black teacher I had ever had. I thought out of everyone, she would understand. To this day, I still believe that she did. I just think she wanted to protect me from the consequences of what I was dangerously insinuating.

After my failed experience at trying to describe what was covert racism without even knowing how to spell "microaggression," I learned to silence the part of me that kept raising the race card and started listening to the voice in my head that was saying that not everything was about race and that some things were just my own fault, Black or not. While this "no excuses" mentality may work for a competitive bodybuilder, for an impressionable seven-year-old, it can soon start to make you feel like you can never do anything right. I had a close friend who was always really critical of everything I did. She showered me with daily doses of passive aggressiveness—things like how my parents should have packed me wheat instead of white bread for lunch and how she was worried about which American Girl doll I would be able to play with when I went to her house. There was another freckle-faced girl, whose last name was well-known in the community, who told me one day that I couldn't be the line leader because "Black people don't get to be at the front of the line." I remember my face getting hot and my palms feeling sweaty. It felt like she had just exposed a well-kept secret, let the cat out of the bag, and said something that they all had been thinking but would never dare say aloud. I felt a sense of paralyzing embarrassment as a pitiful silence rang out loudly from teachers and students alike. For the first time, I had felt the true weight of my skin. It was heavy—almost too heavy to carry.

The next year, I moved into my local school district and attended public school for the first time, where I was met with larger classes, more math, and fewer field trips. In the classroom, we were divided into color groups based off our reading comprehension levels. After flexing my muscles on the reading test, I landed myself a spot in the blue group, the highest level there was. While I was one of three Black students in my entire class, I was the only Black kid in the group. I didn't mind, considering I was so eager to learn new material and get ahead of the other kids that I didn't even notice most of the time. I lived for the moments when I saw a student working on a worksheet that my group had done days before and I could confidently present them with the answer and the exact reason I knew it was right. After a while, I noticed that the teachers started purposely sitting me next to kids in the lower-level reading groups and instructing me on how to "guide" them to the answer instead of just giving it to them. It was a little less fun, but I had already had a lot of practice helping Amir, my autistic younger brother, with his math homework, so I knew just what to do. I didn't mind the task, so I took a break from pushing ahead in the curriculum and started taking steps back to help guide some other students along the right path. Granted, it was only elementary school, and there wasn't much further to go beyond times tables and compound sentences, but the experience further reinforced my sense that I had to make myself useful in every classroom setting, even if it was at the expense of my own progress. The next two years, I was put into the inclusion, or "mixed," classrooms alongside kids with differently abled learning styles, where I did more guiding, helping, and reteaching. My parents, always willfully prepared to advocate on my behalf, brought it to the school's attention and couldn't help but suggest that this method of peer-learning had negative racial implications. Why was I responsible for teaching other students? Why wasn't my learning and development being prioritized? Would they expect the same of a gifted white student? They knew that I would never complain, but they could not stand the idea of my not being challenged to my fullest potential because I could be more useful helping someone else. I agreed with them, but would never let my teachers know that. I did not want them to think I was angry or upset with anyone because I wasn't.

In middle school, I was finally able to just blend in. Other than sending math homework answers to my friend group that I only hung out with once a year, no one really needed me for anything. It was kind of awkward and lonely, but I figured that being sort of invisible was better than being used, so I worked with it. I put my hair in the same modest bun and colored headband every day, forcefully slicking up the pieces in the back that were suffering from breakage. I tolerated non-black students spewing out the *n-word* left and right and made sure not to show any signs of visible discomfort. One day, one of my friends told me that sometimes, she "forgot" that I was Black. She said she knew it when she looked at me, but just thinking about it, she sometimes just forgot. I wanted to respond and tell her that was kind of the whole point. Instead, I just laughed along with her.

Two months into my freshman year, I received a letter from the head basketball coach at a private school. She wrote that she had seen me play at a Showcase event and wanted me to come tour the school and hopefully attend next fall. With my transcript, she was sure I would get in and it would be affordable for me and my family. She was right. I got accepted in March of 2018 and started my sophomore year there in September.

From the start, it was a dream come true. I had so much freedom, the food was great, and people I didn't even know smiled and greeted me in the hallways. The dress code made me feel professional, and in my classes, everyone around me took their learning seriously. We had riveting discussions in my English class where I felt like I got smarter every day. I found a group of friends who were really down to earth and not snobby at all, like I expected most people to be. I even started being featured in the promo videos and ads talking about the school culture, hugging and high-fiving my teammates, and flipping through the pages of a book in one of the new study spaces.

All of these activities distracted me from seeing that I had never really come to terms with my Blackness. I knew that I did not want to be white, nor was I ashamed to be Black, but it was just something that I kind of forgot about because it didn't seem to have a place in the environment I was in. I had gone there to play basketball, after all, not to think about what it meant to be Black. Plus, everyone around me already knew it. They just weren't talking about it because it didn't make a difference to them either way, or so I told myself. They didn't see color, I rationalized, so they would have treated me the same if I were red, purple, green, pink, or sure, even Black. Right?

I continued on in blissful ignorance, letting myself forget about race and making sure I didn't do anything to remind anyone, which meant hair neatly braided every week, collar folded and ironed cleanly, and knees and elbows always moisturized and never ashy. I spent two years slowly separating myself from the negative connotations associated with my skin.

Then the summer of 2020 happened. Back-to-back tragedies struck innocent people and made headlines day after day. Stories of injustice cycled on repeat as the virus that turned cities like mine into "red-zones" kept us locked inside and tethered to the TV to view it all. With each new story, the pattern became more and more clear; no matter who you were, the majority's view of you as a person of color would always impact the way you lived your life, and in some cases, whether or not you deserved to. I felt discouraged, and honestly, guilty, for letting myself forget that there was a "real" world outside the sparkly confines of my closed campus. I thought back to my readings and textbooks and wondered where between the pages of the first Thanksgiving and the American Revolution they had forgotten to include anything that could have prepared me for this—something that dug deeper than a blurb on Rosa Parks or a picture of Martin Luther King Jr., or maybe

Malcolm X. There should have at least been a warning sign, a disclaimer, that read, "This is not just history. It's actually still happening."

I felt like I had to make up for lost time. When the protests broke out near my city, I begged and ultimately convinced my parents to let me attend just *one* of them. Finally, one day, I laced up my shoes, strapped on a visor and mask, and marched out to the center of the Boston Common alongside my dad and two brothers. As we sat on a park bench waiting for the march to begin, I remember feeling, surprisingly, a little embarrassed. Looking around, I saw an overwhelming number of white faces. We were some of the few if not the only Black people in our general vicinity. I started to sense that all-too-familiar silent pity floating in the atmosphere and surrounding us on the bench. My skin felt heavy again, but this time it was almost as if I were wearing the weight of all of their guilt combined. I did not expect to feel this way. In fact, I even grew upset with myself for almost wanting to go home. I tightly clutched the sign I had made from a plaster ceiling tile the night before as a familiar voice in my head told me to tuck it between my legs to hide the bold text on the front that read, "Being black is not a crime." I did not want to draw any more of their attention. Suddenly, someone yelled, "Say his name!" from across the lawn. It was time. I picked up my sign, hoisted it high above my head, and let out a bellow as I moved toward the speaker. This time, I was not holding back.

Watchful eyes followed as my dad, brothers, and I took a spot on the hill where the march was set to begin. The crowd fell silent as the passionate words of a young, Black girl who looked not much older than myself echoed in the thick, summer air. Just as she was finishing her speech, I turned around to see my dad speaking to a middle-aged white guy holding a boxy microphone with a "CBS" logo on it. He said he was from WBZ News and wanted each of us to speak on the local news channel when they would be going live in a few minutes. I felt a wave of anxiety rush over me as I imagined my neighbors, classmates, relatives, coaches, and just about everyone else in the city of Boston seeing my face on their TV screens. But when my brother passed me the microphone and the cameraman focused the lens directly between my eyes, the words came spewing out of me like a shaken-up bottle of Coke: "This is my life," I said when asked why I had chosen to attend the protest. "I can't take off the color of my skin, and I can never escape this reality. If I have to sit here and be affected by this every single day, then every other human should care about it, too. I'm not going to stop talking about it. I need to be here, and I need to have my voice heard." I handed the microphone back to the reporter with trembling hands and looked back again at my dad, who had that typical, proud-parent look on his face. I knew I had just done something right.

I returned to school in September 2020, assuming we had each had our own sort of epiphany, however large or small it may have been. But somehow, the campus felt eerily and awkwardly quiet. It was like standing in the eye of a storm, trying desperately to stay safe and sound while everything around us was being uprooted and swirled into oblivion. Two years ago, this might have made me feel safe and understood, but now it felt like a cover-up. We had all just witnessed the last seconds of a person's life on the same screens that we use to take selfies and play Candy Crush, and it seemed like any mention of the fact was forbidden, banished to the outside, or vacuum-sealed in the enclosed, sound-proofed walls of the Students of Color Affinity Group.

I had gotten used to being just about the only Black student in each of my classes and understood this meant my classmates and I experienced the world very differently and would not always see eye to eye. What I was not prepared for was the overwhelming sense of defensive hostility that seemed to slap me in the face as I walked through the hallways. In one particular class, this subtle antagonism was heightened as our left-leaning teacher would occasionally address social, economic, and racial issues that were relevant to the class lesson plan. The students' leading questions and underhanded comments spoke volumes on how they had chosen to view the events of the prior two months. When the Capitol riots broke out in early January, one student rhetorically asked how those "protests" were different from the Black Lives Matter riots that had ravaged the nation all summer. I knew better than to take the bait; they knew what I stood for, and I was not about to be the angry Black girl who took on the task of trying to explain racism to white people. After that, my teacher decided it was best to conduct a change to the seating chart, and I ended up in the farthest corner of the classroom near the windows and heating vents. I sat there, mostly in silence, often feeling uncomfortable, targeted, and deeply alone. Most days, I didn't even feel like going to school, but I was not about to allow them to win. Instead, I chose to put my head down, retreat deeply into myself, and dissociate from my surroundings.

I later learned that there was a term for the sort of numbness that I felt every time I walked through the doors of the school. It's called double-consciousness. W.E.B. Dubois first used it to describe the plight faced by African Americans in the oppressive society to which they had been forced to assimilate after being "freed" from slavery. Essentially, it means we live two conflicting existences, one in which we might have a sense of self-worth and identity and another that makes us look back at ourselves through its own lens of contempt, diminishes our self-image, then asks us how it feels to be the problem. I had spent the summer becoming conscious of my role in a nation that did not seem to value the lives—not the culture, the sports teams, or the music, but the lives—of people who looked like me, and still there was a feeling that I was supposed to just fall into this safe space and forget.

I know now that you cannot expect people to understand something they have never experienced, but it is enough to ask that they at least acknowledge your reality and not try to make you look at your situation through their own rose-colored lens. This country works really well for some people, but it has a tendency to forget about others and push their needs to the back-burner. Being one of the "others" has made me understand how important it is that we find our own sense of worth and dignity and not measure ourselves by impossible standards that do not account for our fullest and truest selves. At the times when I have felt most alone, I have found comfort in members of the faculty who sympathized with what I was going through, and made it clear that they always supported and believed in me even when it felt like the whole world was against me. With the encouragement of the Director of Diversity, who is basically the only Black authority figure we students of color can all trust and go to for advice, I decided to write my public speaking assignment on my struggle with identity as a young, Black woman, focusing in on my complex experience with the culture of the school.

On the day of the speech, my legs shook violently beneath the podium as I filled the pin-drop silence of the room with four minutes and forty-six seconds of my truest, most unapologetic honesty. Toward the end, I decided to address the students of color with some advice that I wish someone would have told me when I first enrolled. I told them that as Black people, we have to find ways to define ourselves rather than searching for our purpose and identity in a society that will measure our worth by what it can take from us. As Toni Morrison once said, "Freeing yourself is one thing, claiming ownership of that freed self is another." What does claiming ownership mean for me? Well, I just did it. This is me, and I am taking control of my own story.

Chocolate City

LATRELLE N. CHASE

I was born on an army base in Maryland. I spent my young years in Washington, DC, proper and Prince George's County, Maryland. I'm a proud Black DC/Maryland/Virginia (DMV) girl—one of those girls who says "errybody," "errything," and "Murrrrrland." I'm so DC. I'm mambo sauce and go-go music DC. I'm Chocolate City DC. I'm at the Stone Souled picnic in the park DC. Wilmers Park for the go-gos in the summer. I am *that* Black girl. I was raised at a time when Black excellence was on full display through education, jobs, real estate purchases, and more. It was not foreign to see folks who looked like me winning. It also wasn't foreign to see Black people in abundance all the time. My parents bought their first home when they were in their early 20s. They then went on to build a house from the ground up by their 30s. My mom was an entrepreneur in addition to her full-time day job. My parents always encouraged my creative side. My hair was colored a really cool shade of aubergine by the time I was 14 years old. My hair stayed in fantasy colors when fantasy colors weren't cool, normal, or acceptable. I have always been the type to set my own trends, be it vintage clothing or eclectic jewelry mixed in with the latest fashions. I always wanted things that would cause me to stand out and stand apart.

I started off high school briefly at the famed Duke Ellington School of the Arts in DC, where I met this fine dude at 14 (who eventually became my forever boyfriend). I was not really about the intensity of the performing arts school life, so I ended up transferring and then later graduating from Surrattsville High School in Clinton, Maryland, a suburb right outside of DC in Prince George's County. Fun fact: Prince George's County is considered to be one of the wealthiest counties in the country for African Americans. At Surrattsville, I found myself in a very diverse high school that was about 60 percent Black. We didn't really talk about race too much. Looking back, I think that we thought it didn't even really matter. You were either classified as Black or white. I realized as an adult that wasn't really true. We were kids, and we loved each other. We argued. We fought. We made up. We loved each other again. It was definitely a little Pleasantville-type experience where everyone pretty much got along and judged you for you, not for what you looked like. Or so I naively thought. I went on to college in Alabama at Tuskegee University. I really had no fear of going to the Deep South. I was attending a historically Black college or university (HBCU). Attending an HBCU was not even a conversation. The only choice was *which* HBCU I would attend. My classmates, with their varied life experiences, looked like me. There I continued to see the Black excellence to which I'd been accustomed my entire life.

In 1996, I married my forever boyfriend and high school sweetheart and relocated to Boston to be with him. He had recently graduated from college and had some great opportunities in New England. Everything was about to change. The first lesson that relocating to Boston taught me was what being Black in America really means. I had no idea being Black in America is *not* the same as being Black in DC. If I'm being honest, being Black in Boston is not the same as being Black in Massachusetts. Minority is a word I'd heard my entire life. I know what the word means. I knew I was a minority because someone said I was. However, it wasn't until I relocated to Massachusetts that I became painfully aware. Before I was a minority because of my race. It was almost like a nonfactor, if you will. But now, I was a minority in the textbook definition of the word minority. It was a strange feeling. It was a new feeling. It was an uncomfortable feeling. I am one who prides myself on being from DC. I believed that growing up in DC had been my training ground on being a young Black woman and every trial that would ever come my way. It was disheartening to realize that my beloved hometown had taught me so little about how to navigate spaces where you are the odd man out. I just assumed this was how the whole country operated. It was so foreign to me to be in a place where often I was the only Black person in a restaurant, the only Black person in social settings, the only Black person at work. I'd never been here before. The real struggle for me was not *being* the only Black person, it was being treated as if I somehow wasn't good enough to be there or that I didn't belong. That became something that made me angry and unsettled. It caused me a tremendous amount of anxiety and left me unsure of everything that I thought I knew about not just being Black, but simply being LaTrelle.

As I began my new life in Boston, it was a little rocky getting hired, but eventually I landed a gig. I can still vividly hear my coworkers mocking my accent. If you've ever been to the mid-Atlantic region, you know that DC folks (particularly melanated ones) have a very distinct accent. Some Northerners insist that it's a Southern accent. Technically, yes, being below the Mason Dixon line is Southern. But it's truly not a Southern accent. I really didn't mind much at first because I also found their accents particularly amusing. "Pahk your cah in Hahvid yahd." I soon realized they weren't really mocking my accent. Rather, they were mocking my intelligence. From the silly nicknames like Forrest Gump to questioning everything I said and did, my anger was now reaching a fever pitch. This wasn't about Ebonics or speaking African-American Vernacular English (AAVE). No, these people actually thought I was stupid because of a twang. They had no problem expressing that. After a few "come to Jesus" conversations, I quietly exited that workplace. I moved on to another job, and the same thing happened. But I knew who I was; humble brag, I am brilliant! So I started speaking up. When my boss would say things, which I now know are microaggressions, I would respond. He once tried to explain the mailing lists to me that we purchased; he thought that I wouldn't recognize names like *Forbes* and *Newsweek*. So he said something to the effect of "Oh, so it would be like *Essence* and *Ebony*. You read those, no?" I did. But I also read *Forbes* and *Newsweek*, and I let him know that. When he would speak about his boat or other things, I'd chime in about my experiences growing up on the water. I grew up in an upper-middle-class family, and my grandparents owned a boat. I remember him being very surprised, as if my Blackness could not have allowed me to experience such things. Now let me be clear, *things* don't make you Black or deserving. But being Black doesn't make you undeserving, and there should not be assumptions made about your experiences. Black people are not monolithic. We don't all have the same experiences. Once I realized that, I found my voice. I stopped shrinking back. I stopped downplaying how dope I am. Finding my voice served me well over the years in career shifts and moves. I was able to take the lessons that I learned in DC and marry them with the hits I'd taken upon my relocation to Massachusetts. I kept moving and growing.

In my early 30s, I reconnected with a former work colleague and stumbled upon a new career as a public school career and vocational technical education (CVTE) teacher. I couldn't believe it. Teaching was not something that I planned or even really saw myself doing, especially not full time. Becoming a teacher was one of the most welcome and beautiful surprises of my life. I found my passion and mission working with teenagers. This particular teaching job didn't require a degree, so I easily settled into a groove.

I was very surprised to see how few vocational teachers of color there were in Massachusetts. Remember, I came from a place where whatever you saw the majority race doing, you saw Black folks doing. So it was odd to only see a handful of Black people teaching trades. There was a particular professional development workshop at my school, and the facilitator asked for someone to share out loud to the group. I quickly volunteered. One of my coworkers remarked how articulate I was. I thanked him. He said it again, and then again. After the fourth "Wow, I can't believe how articulate you are," I felt my anger reach a boiling point. I asked him what exactly was so hard to believe about it. Articulate is never a compliment to a grown woman, especially a Black woman. He told me that I was overreacting. I assured him that I was not. I let him know that he should be alarmed if I was *not* well spoken. To tell someone that they have a way with words, that they are a masterful storyteller, is absolutely not the same as telling a fully grown woman that she is articulate. I naively believed that some of the microaggressions I dealt with in my 20s would not follow me into public school education. I was simply flabbergasted that another educated person really did not see the issue with any of this. From that day forward, I vowed that my approach and response to microaggressions would change. And they did. They changed for the better, or so I believed.

In 2014, I returned to college after dropping out in 1994. I earned a Bachelor of Arts in Multidisciplinary Studies. Shortly after that, a Master of Education in Curriculum Writing and Instruction. I was attending school full time, teaching full time, and also running the hair salon that I owned. I was quietly making moves with my education so that I could make moves in the educational world. My degrees allowed me to find myself doing much more in the Career/Vocational Technical Education (CVTE) world, just as I had planned. While doing some independent work on an accreditation team in education, I found myself as I often do, the only person of color. I was the only Black person, and definitely the only person with pink hair. I was excited for the opportunity. This was my first time on this type of assignment. My excitement quickly faded as I found myself ostracized. I watched over 30 people from various parts of New England, most of whom had never met each other, easily interact. As I tried to ease my way into conversations, nobody seemed to be really interested in engaging with me. As we continued our work in the coming days, I found myself alone. There was one woman with whom I was partnered who was technologically challenged, so she did interact with me, but only when absolutely necessary. As part of our teamwork, each member of the team did two oral presentations of their findings. I watched as each person got up to do their presentation. The other team members would listen but continue with their writing and work on their laptops. When it was my turn to present, at least eight other people had gone. I noticed that many people closed their laptops and turned to face me. I remember thinking, "That's odd." Once I was done with my presentation, one of my teammates looked over at me and said, "You're really articulate." At least four more people repeated that or some variation. I was triggered. I was so upset that I called my mom to vent. I always remember her words. "LaTrelle, your job is to tear down stereotypes one idiot at a time." Every night after we finished our work, team members would get together for a nightcap. I wasn't included the first two nights. After my presentation, magically, I was no longer invisible. "Oh, LaTrelle, come hang out with us." I declined. I did, however, end up speaking with a guy around my age from Connecticut. We spoke for a long time about race, ethnicity, being Black in America, being Black in academia, and being Black in vocational education. Rather, I should say I talked and he listened. The next day, he thanked me and told me that I had challenged him and he had to check some of his biases after our conversation.

Fast forward to the next year, I was on another visiting team. This time around, I was feeling very confident. I knew what to expect, and more importantly, I knew what to do and *how* to do it. I had put all the previous year's nonsense in the back of my head. Then it came quickly rushing back as I was met with the same resistance. I sought out the leader and offered my knowledge as this team was made up of a lot of first timers, as I'd been before. He declined my offer. It was eventually time for presentations, and the first presenter wasn't quite prepared. I again offered. The leader reluctantly accepted. I did my presentation. The room was quiet for a minute. It felt like the longest 45-60 seconds of my life. Then I heard, "So, we'll use LaTrelle's presentation as an example going forward." I smiled big on the inside, as I remembered my mother's words the year before. The next day, I was having breakfast, and the waitress said, "My daughter loved you." I looked around to see who she was speaking to. She told me that as she was driving her daughter and friends to school that day, they were talking about the really cool Black lady with the blue hair. Oh, yeah, this time around, my hair was electric blue. She said, "As you can imagine, we don't see a lot of Black ladies with blue hair around here."

These days, I mostly find myself being the only Black woman at the table. It doesn't intimidate me. It never did. But it did cause me to be worried about whether it intimidated others. Because I was (and if I am being honest, sometimes still am) worried about intimidating others, I allowed my voice to be diminished. Nobody asked me to do this. I did it. Why did I do this, you ask? I did it because I allowed my perceptions of other people's thoughts to take up residence in my head. I have learned and am still learning that other people's thoughts of me really aren't my concern. I believed until very recently that the way I allow my voice to be diminished is by apologizing for my words before I even verbalize them. I still struggle with often saying "I'm sorry" as a precursor to my thoughts. Honestly, I often say I am sorry as a precursor to the truth. I don't say it because I am sorry. I say it because I am, like many of you, conscious of not coming across as the angry Black woman. Saying "I'm sorry" when I am really not should not be my modus operandi. I was on a work call just a few months ago, and there was a conversation that was a bit uncomfortable. There was an elephant in the room that needed to be addressed, and that elephant was race related. I tried to ignore that nagging feeling in the pit of my stomach. But try as I might, it just would not go away. Sometimes as the only Black person at the table, you are able to see blind spots that others may not see, specifically when the blind spots are about race. In this instance, that was exactly what was happening. The idea that was presented was well intentioned but had the propensity to end up a disastrous misstep. I feared that the repercussions would far outweigh any of the benefits. Once it became clear that the nagging feeling was not going away, I spoke up. I can still remember the words, "I'm sorry to bring this up, but…" and ending with "Again, I apologize for having to say this." I was not sorry at all. Why did I feel the need to say either? Ironically, it was a non-person of color who said, "Let me start by saying you don't ever need to apologize for speaking up. I appreciate you drawing attention to something that I honestly never would have thought of. So please do not apologize." I remember chuckling a bit to myself on the inside and thinking, "Yeah, I really wasn't apologizing" but also realizing that he was correct. As marginalized people, we have to stop apologizing in those instances. Say what you have to say. Stand in the truth, that's that.

I have come to understand that I have a greater responsibility in the workplace. I have a greater responsibility at the proverbial table. My responsibility is not to represent every Black person. It is not to push the narrative that the Black experience is a monolith. However, I do believe that my responsibility is to show up every day being the best version of me that I am. My responsibility is to never be satisfied with being the one seat at the table. Growing up among so many Black people in the DMV area did not adequately prepare me for my new life. Therefore, there have been some missteps along the way. I have doubted myself. I have not been true to myself. I have toned down my Blackness when I did not recognize that my Blackness was not some mistake of which to be ashamed or to hide, but rather that it is my superpower and it should be celebrated loudly and proudly. Even though I felt my beloved hometown did not adequately prepare me for the subtle racism that is embedded not only in the fabric of New England but also the fabric of the United States of America, I can now say that Massachusetts taught me some real lessons. Talk about on-the-spot training. Massachusetts taught me grit. It taught me perseverance. It taught me how to truly be bodacious in the face of naysayers. The DMV raised me. Massachusetts grew me up in a way that I never thought possible. This place in which I swore I would not spend more than two years has taught me some twenty-five years later to navigate difficult spaces and situations. It has taught me that it is up to me to create seats for others who look like me. It has taught me that it is absolutely okay to teach young Black and Brown girls that they are amazing; to teach them that minority is not a word about which to be embarrassed. It is not a word allowed to be used to diminish you and all of your amazing magical abilities.

These days, I use my voice to amplify the voices of those who look like me. I use my voice to change the narrative—not only my personal narrative, but *the* narrative. I use my voice to be a change agent in the vocational education world. I use my voice to tear down stereotypes, one idiot at a time.

I Had to Die in Order to Truly Live

CHARMAINE L. ARTHUR

"Acting like it doesn't exist doesn't heal."
– Soledad O'Brien

While my career as an advocate, speaker, and trainer spans over 28 years, it came about after an abrupt detour from fashion design. I attended college for fashion design and cosmetology after high school believing this path was my life's purpose. After working in the fashion and sales industry for a number of years, I had a desire to work in my community because of what I experienced when I was pregnant with my own son. The people who were hired to assist you with pregnancy and childbirth somehow always felt like they were the enemy. I wanted to treat other women like human beings. My entry into the human services field was as a case manager for women of child-bearing age.

I took on this role during a time when the infant mortality rate amongst women of color was extremely high. I advocated for women to receive quality health care, food, housing, and emotional support. I also worked with a population of women who suffered from drug addiction. My job positioned me against a system poised to work against women, tearing down their identity and humanity. I struggled many days in my role because I saw the light go out in the eyes of many women. Some days it scared me knowing how easily I could find myself in a similar position. Writing this piece has allowed me to reflect and recognize that this very fear was my reality. I had become some of what I saw in the women for whom I advocated, a woman struggling with her own identity and self-worth.

Eventually, I left that role and transitioned to working with youth. I remember my interview as if it was yesterday. The director had interviewed several people, and my boss at the time encouraged me to apply for the position. I interviewed and got hired immediately. While I had some experience serving in the community, this role was when I began to acknowledge my roots in service being developed. I held several positions in the youth development and educational field that allowed me to work directly with our young women. I provided life skills and character development programming for elementary, middle, and high school students. During this career move, I had the opportunity to go back to college and receive my bachelor's degree in Sociology.

I continued to persevere with challenges in the human services field. I was offered many opportunities to train practitioners and direct service staff. I served as a grants manager for the management and annual distribution of over $500,000 in multi-year grants to program partners. I trained and facilitated in the areas of diversity, multiculturalism, domestic and teen violence, sexuality, and HIV/AIDS awareness and prevention. My nonprofit career continued to expand as it allowed me to develop budgets for departments, hire and train staff, design and implement programs, legislate, and research and write policies that would impact the educational progress of Black and Brown youth. In 2005, I used those skills to launch Ladies First, a program serving middle school and high school girls who were disconnected from services and resources necessary to support their personal and emotional growth. I did not know that my gifts would align me with having a clearer understanding of my purpose.

Ladies First helped Black and Brown girls focus on their self-esteem, image, and identity. Little girls of color are too often bombarded with mixed messages about their identity. They grow into adults who continuously struggle throughout life with issues surrounding their identity. Our program recognized that childhood issues with identity would continue to be a struggle for many of our girls as they internalized the most damaging manifestations of racism and the myths and stereotypes about their beauty and intelligence. Colorism was a stereotype on which we focused and was an important topic of discussion with the girls in our program.

The Oxford English Dictionary defines colorism as "prejudice or discrimination against individuals with a dark skin tone, typically among people of the same ethnic or racial group." While many of us understand racism as being a *them against us* power play rooted in prejudice due to skin tone, colorism is a lesser known, almost subliminal stereotype mainly performed *against us by us*. Similar to the effects of racism, this form of prejudice also includes the power dynamic that has social implications. Our focus on color with the girls came as I witnessed first-hand the impact of colorism within Black and Brown communities from which our girls came and realized that I, too, had my own struggles with my skin tone.

Thoughts of colorism have led me to reflect on a show I used to watch on TV during much of the 1990s. The show was about four professional Black women living in Brooklyn, New York. The women were all beautiful in shape, style, size, skin color, and intellect. The show focused on their lives, relationships, and their careers. One of the women, whom I admired the most, was the chocolate beauty of the crew and a successful lawyer. She was feisty, witty, and humorous. As much as I enjoyed her character, I never thought she realized how beautiful she was. I also felt like she worked harder than her peers to be seen and heard. However, when she spoke up, she came across as aggressive to many. I always got the feeling that she was trying to find her position amongst her friends, even though she was amazingly brilliant and beautiful. In retrospect, I wonder if what I saw in that particular character was a reflection of how I saw myself. As a dark-skinned woman,

I encountered a number of exchanges growing up that helped sow the seed of self-hate.

I came to America from Trinidad and Tobago at the age of seven and struggled to adapt to a culture that assumed everybody with an accent was from Jamaica. There was a general lack of knowledge about West Indians and how diverse we are. As a result, I was relegated to being Jamaican. For the first few years after our arrival, my mother home-schooled me, so when I finally started public school, I was placed in advanced classes immediately. In elementary school, my teachers would call on me to speak and to present my work. When I spoke, my accent would stand out, and I would be teased by some of my peers. It was not long before I began to rebel in school and did not want to speak or present in class because I hated the attention my accent caused. I quickly learned how mean children could be, especially children from America. As I went through middle school, my accent was not as thick because I had adapted to some of the culture.

As a preteen, I developed a love for fashion, hair, and dance and began to express myself through those mediums. Having presumably shed the elephant in the room, my accent, I began to consider myself like many of my friends. Then things began to change at the peak of adolescence. In the eighth grade, I got into a physical fight with a boy who decided he would make fun of my skin color. Interestingly enough, he was a darker shade of brown than me. I could not believe the words that came out of his mouth. I thought we were friends, but on that day, many things changed for me. It was the first time that I saw my skin color as an issue to somebody else. I grew up in a home with both of my parents. My mother was a beautiful chocolate brown woman, and my father was what some in my family would call yellow. He was a lighter brown tone. I don't ever recall skin color being a big topic of discussion at the dinner table. My siblings and I were all shades of brown, and my parents did not prefer one shade over another. The idea of the depth of one's melanin being an issue to anyone was foreign to me.

My circle of friends from middle through high school were also all shades of melanin, but I was always the darkest in the crew. In high school, it felt more obvious than ever. There was attention given to the lighter-skinned girls in school, who differed greatly from the girls who were darker skinned. There was this false assumption that dark-skinned girls were mean and angry. Many were labeled easy and also ugly just because of the shade of their skin. I was an athlete in high school, so I became friends with many of the boys on the sports teams. We had sports in common—nothing more, nothing less—but for some reason the rumors surfaced that it was more. Before long, I was hearing that I was sleeping around with the whole team, despite your girl was still a virgin in high school, even after prom night. Those experiences caused me to develop a hard external core as I grew older. I was not only witty with words, but I was also quick with my hands. Eventually, I began to live up to the stereotypes that label us as "angry black women." I think what many fail to realize is that our anger is valid because, too many times, we are made to feel less than and are expected to bottle it all up and not talk about how it affects us. I was judged in many ways based on the shade of my melanin—something that was once unimaginable to me.

My experiences in high school began to shape me into somebody I did not like. I was constantly angry and aggressive. My outspoken and aggressive tone was off-putting to many and had a negative effect on my relationships with friends and family. The times I was called out about my skin tone, assumptions about my sexuality, and even my mood all became sources of embarrassment and shame. I hated to be embarrassed! If I felt that someone was trying to shame me, I would lash out.

I recall an incident I had with one of my teachers. One day, a friend who played softball was playing an away game and invited me to join her on the team bus. We honestly did not know that we needed permission from her coach for me to travel with them. I figured that being an athlete myself was enough. As we sat on the bus, the coach came on and let it be known that I could not travel with them on the bus to the game. I was angry and embarrassed because she had just yelled at me in front of everybody. That was enough of a trigger, and I did what I always thought was the best way to respond when I felt embarrassed. I ended up cussing the coach out! As a result, I was kicked off of the bus and went home. The next day in school, I had to report to her classroom to discuss what had happened on the bus. Just imagine, this coach was about four-eleven, petite, and a brown-skinned fireball who had zero time for hot headed students. That day, the coach read me like a book. I remember her words like it was yesterday. She said to me, "I am over 50 years old. Don't you ever in your lifetime think you can speak to me that way. What the hell is wrong with you?" I remember how surprised I was to hear those words come out of her mouth. What also stood out to me was her ability to read the situation as something deeper than lashing out and give me grace by not recommending suspension. Instead, she asked me to come to her classroom each day and spend time with her. I gained a great deal of respect for the coach that year because she chose to work with me and look past my hard exterior. She told me she saw something in me that I did not see in myself: power and beauty. I remember her asking me why I was so angry. I believe I responded with an "I don't know." She responded, "Well, we are going to find out together." In subsequent years, this woman also coached me in other sports. I remained accountable to her as an athlete and a young person seeking to look at life with a different perspective. She loved and supported me as I grew and corrected my mouth and actions when I needed correction.

High school was a bittersweet experience for me. In addition to some of my struggles with colorism and the negative assumptions that followed, I also had a strict upbringing. I was not allowed to date boys during most of my high school years. I was surprised when my parents allowed me to get a part-time job. I remember wanting a house phone for my room, and my parents agreed that I could have the phone if I was able to pay for it. I ended up taking a part-time job in a shoe store.

Working in the shoe store allowed me to meet a lot of people. I especially liked it when cute guys would come in the store looking for church shoes or prom shoes when prom season came along. Too often, I would meet people who would compliment my style of clothing but would also give me backhanded compliments about my looks. I heard statements like "You are attractive for a dark-skinned girl." I remember not knowing how to feel the first time I heard that. I questioned whether I should be pissed off or act like it did not offend me. Unfortunately, it became a regular occurrence at the hands of Black men, in particular those who shared or had complexions darker than mine. The dislike I had toward darker-skinned Black men grew from the constant slight I experienced from them. I began to lose interest in dating dark-skinned men. I definitely believe high school is what kicked off my campaign to *only* date lighter-skinned men.

I met my first real boyfriend during my senior year of high school at the shoe store where I worked. This young man was very light skinned. He was Puerto Rican with hazel eyes and blondish-colored hair. I was the dark-skinned sister who now refused to date dark-skinned men and was beyond happy to go to prom with my Puerto Rican date. I learned to hate the shade of my skin because of how my own people made me feel. When we talk about our first experiences of hate, isolation, and discrimination, most people expect you to say it began with an interaction with white people. Well that ain't my story! As a matter of fact, for a short period of time, I dated outside of my race. I had an identity crisis for a very long time and did not realize it until several years later. I was not content with who I saw in the mirror daily. I styled my hair in a very Eurocentric way—straight weaves that honestly did not match my natural curly hair. In order for my natural hair to match the straight hair, I had to relax my hair. I fell deep into the false belief for Black women, that the Eurocentric definition of beauty was what real beauty was about. Although my mother did not verbalize it on a daily basis, I remember her not liking hairstyles that were close to curly or kinky-style afros. Ironically, she came to this country with a beautiful curly afro, but she, too, began to use a relaxer, "the creamy crack." The terminology came about because we became addicted to straightening our hair to achieve other people's standards of beauty. As I think about my mother's interaction with her natural hair, there was a dislike that she showed for it. I never understood until I learned that my mother also struggled with her identity as a dark-skinned immigrant woman. I learned that her pain did not come from strangers but from within her own circle. My mother shared with me stories about not being liked by some of my father's siblings because of the shade of her skin. There were experiences she eventually shared that allowed me to understand why she responded to certain things in such a condescending way, like me desiring to wear my natural hair in an afro. We had learned to internalize the self-hate that we had experienced from others. This treatment came about by strangers and people in our circles, whether they realized it or not.

As I became established as a career woman and created a name for myself, I was still defining my worth based on other people's definitions of beauty. My struggles with self-love enabled me to make a number of bad decisions in relationships. I also struggled with my identity, and it impacted how I showed up in the world. I would meet dark-skinned men who liked me for me, but since I was not sure of my own self, I would reject them. I remember the day I met this dark brother at a club. He was the poster boy for "the darker the berry." This young man pursued me for months, and eventually, we started dating. My relationship with him was not just a romantic one—we became the best of friends. He treated me like a queen. He loved everything about me and always told me that. I was not accustomed to direct expressions of love growing up as a little girl. This in no way means I was not loved at home. My father was present in my life and was an amazing provider, but he was not an emotional provider. So much of what I learned about healthy relationships and self-love was through much trial and error.

When I launched Ladies First in 2005, I knew I wanted to focus on self-love and self-confidence. I wanted our young women to learn how to rediscover their internal and external beauty regardless of their skin tone. I wanted them to learn to walk in a power that only they could find within, and I wanted them to learn to heal from the pain of words. As I worked with young women, I realized that the little girl in me had not healed. The little girl in me was still angry and hurt. Even though I received accolades for the work I was doing in my community, I was still struggling internally. I still struggled with my identity. I woke up many days wearing a mask for the world and still fighting those self-loathing demons. During my time managing Ladies First, I was introduced to a funding opportunity to support the work I was doing with girls. The opportunity introduced me to an organization called the Women's Theological Center (WTC). WTC was a program addressing issues of social justice from a faith and spiritual perspective. They facilitated transformational change through cultivating the leadership of Black, Indigenous, women of color and diverse communities. WTC is where I began to learn about self-love through healing from my traumatic experiences. While I learned a lot about my identity growing up with my parents, I did not learn how to confront the pain that caused me much harm until I began my transformational journey. WTC is where I began my own journey to healing. I got the opportunity to attend a weekend retreat on transformational healing. During the retreat, we began to dissect labels that were placed upon us by other people and labels we had placed upon ourselves. It was the first time I experienced a ritual that allowed me to be vulnerable and transparent about my pain. We wrote the labels on a piece of sticky note paper and described the impact the label had on our identity. We were each asked to throw the label in the fire. The label burning ritual symbolized the healing of unresolved issues that I had within myself. This ritual taught me to confront and accept what was, learn to forgive myself and others, and continue to move forward. There were many days where confronting was easy but accepting and forgiving was not. We hear so much that "forgiveness is not for the people who hurt you, it is for yourself." Can I tell you, even though it is a true statement, many times you just cannot forgive. Forgiveness is a process that takes time. It is about extending mercy to those who have brought harm to our lives, even when they do not deserve it. Forgiveness can come with a big emotional price tag, but it is worth the journey.

My journey to healing and reconciling unresolved conflict increased along my walk of faith. As a Christian, I began to learn about what unconditional love truly meant. I grew up in a Pentecostal church. For those who are not familiar with the Pentecostal doctrine, let me give you Wikipedia's definition: "Pentecostals believe that faith must be powerfully experiential, and not something found merely through ritual or thinking. It is energetic and dynamic. Its members believe they are driven by the power of God moving within them." Although Wikipedia is correct, my definition also includes the importance of conversion through the baptism in the Holy Spirit. Being filled with the Holy Spirit means giving the believer strength to endure a Christian life and gifts of the Spirit. During my spiritual journey, I learned a lot, but there are many things I had to unlearn in order to dig deep into my healing. I also went into therapy. One of the things I learned on this journey to healing is the importance of having your faith, your Bible, and your therapist. Healing is removing layers of trauma and pain, and I realized that I could not achieve that solely through a spiritual singing, dancing, and praying Sunday service. I needed a process that pushed me to the core of exposing my pain and to not be fearful of what came forth. Look, healing is painful. It is one of the hardest things that we will ever face, and that is why some people will stay in their pain longer—because they are afraid of what the healing process will expose.

When I received the vision for Facing Our Journey International Ministries, I knew that our vision and mission would involve going beyond the four walls of a church building to reach those who may never come into the church. It would involve seeking to find lost, hurting, and broken people and committing to meet them at their need through healing, transformation, and reconciliation without judgment. Through my work in the community, I launched the Circles of Healing initiative—an initiative that believes in the power of healing and wholeness and its lasting impact on our lives. I cannot begin to tell you the stories that I have heard from our girls and women about the challenges they face daily surviving the loss of a loved one, divorce, racism, colorism, microaggression, abuse, rape, suicide, and more.

As a Black Caribbean woman, mental health counseling was not a daily conversation in my home. We were taught through messaging that we must develop tough skin and fight for our independence—basically, seek to get over it. For many women and girls, this mindset is a normal part of their growth and development, but not a healthy one. Depression was a huge health concern in my life. Mental health, even with all of the knowledge in 2021, still remains stigmatized in many communities of color. Although it does impact women from all walks of life, I have witnessed how cultural norms and historical experiences caused depression to be expressed and addressed differently among Black women. Black women remain one of the most undertreated groups for depression in the United States.

My trauma and pain led me to fall into the stereotype of the "strong Black woman," a belief that teaches many of us that we do not have time to deal with depression. Some women still believe it is only a white experience. The ideology of the strong Black woman teaches us that we are unshakeable, unmovable, unbreakable, and born with strength. Although there is so much truth to that, as I think about the strong women who came before and those who will come after me—my mother, my aunts, my sister, my daughter and granddaughters, and my village. I also know that not addressing our pain and trauma will increase illnesses in our bodies and can kill us faster. I had to learn the importance of self-love, self-confidence, and self-care to be able to teach others in my community about the importance of healing. Despite what I experienced through my own journey, Black women who have more awareness about trauma and pain and acknowledge and own their struggles can overcome, be transformed and heal. My healing was not a magic potion created in somebody else's lab. My healing came through truly knowing, understanding, and accepting who God created me to be. It came by first forgiving myself and forgiving the people who caused harm to the little girl and the adult woman that I became, even if I believe they did not deserve it. I healed through creating rituals of self-care and self-love with daily affirmations of appreciation of myself. Soledad O'Brien's quote "Acting like it doesn't exist doesn't heal" is powerful. Our memories trigger a lot of our pain. The secrets that we keep for fear of exposing others triggers our pain. Don't you get tired of refusing to tell your story because it will expose the harm that other people caused? I host a bi-weekly roundtable on Facebook titled "Pathway to Victory." I created a platform for men and women to share their life's journey with the world. To testify about their pathway to becoming victorious. Remember when we are healing and becoming whole, we are positioned to take back the power that was taken from us. I can no longer allow others to write my narrative. My beauty will never be defined by whether I can pass the paper bag test. In 2021, we are still facing the same issues around colorism and its impact on the Black, Indigenous, and people of color (BIPOC) community and our relationships. The year 2020 heightened the issue even more with the social injustices impacting Black and Brown men, women and children all over the world. I'm reminded of the words from speaker and author Steve Maraboli: "This is my life…my story…my book. I will no longer let anyone else write it; nor will I apologize for the edits I make."

Find Your Black Girl Magical North Star

~~~~~~~~

MALLORY ROSE ST. BRICE

In my 16-year career, I have been fired two times. Yes, *two* times. Despite these firings, which I now know were both blessings in disguise, I have had an otherwise admirable early career. I have worked in senior management and leadership roles within the nonprofit sector in the area of positive youth development. I started in management just a couple years out of college and for over a decade was often one of the youngest staff members and only Black person or Black woman in the office. I've supervised anywhere from one to twenty people at a time and have been recognized by my employers and colleagues as an exemplary manager and leader, particularly for how I approach managing *people*.

My care and attention to managing people has everything to do with how I, as a Haitian American Black woman growing up and living in and around Greater Boston, have experienced the good and bad of being a manager in social justice work. My mom's stories about growing up poor in Haiti, the political turmoil she witnessed, and how she started in the United States often resonated with me and created in me a desire to do work that attempts to break cycles of poverty and ensure economic opportunity for all. My mom, of course, often instilled in me the inalienable value of education, and that, for Black people especially, it can be a tool for upward mobility. I think that my mom wanted my brothers and me to believe, very simply, that all we needed was to get a great education and work hard and we would be okay—that being Black, or a woman, or middle income, would not matter. So it should be no surprise that I am "overeducated." In fact, Black women are becoming the most post-secondary educated group in America. I currently hold a Bachelor of Science in Sociology, a Master of Art in Urban Affairs, and Master of Business Administration in Human Resources Management. All these degrees are my way of saying to white America, "Look at me. I know stuff. Trust me. Believe in me." But my ongoing pursuit of education, both in the classroom, in the workplace, and even in the streets, is also a way that I have had to invest in my own growth and development the way that few employers have and only I can.

As a professional, what has propped me up in the face of explicit racism, microaggressions with a macro impact, imposter syndrome, and frankly, anxiety and depression that are often exacerbated by these experiences are the following three pieces of advice for navigating the workplace as a Black woman: 1) Avoid the cultural fit trap, 2) It's okay to give yourself grace to cry deeply and heal, and 3) You must identify your north star.

Let me back up though and tell you about the *first time* I got fired. I had been working as an administrative coordinator for a community consulting and economic development nonprofit in Boston for about 10 months. It was my first real professional job after completing my undergraduate studies at Suffolk University and after deciding not to go to law school to be either a criminal defense or civil rights attorney and rack up more debt. I had decided that the criminal justice system was totally rigged, and I preferred to do work that was more prevention- and early intervention-focused and that would have an impact on a more systemic level. When I started the job at the consulting firm, I was eager to make my mark on the world like many bright-eyed young adults transcending into adulthood and finding their life's purpose. I was truly honored for the opportunity to work for this reputable company that had affiliations with Harvard University and some of the greatest minds in business and economics. But it turned out that I hated that job. The reason is that I felt I lacked adequate onboarding, coaching, and mentorship that met me where I was as a Black woman and recent college graduate to be successful. They threw me in the deep end and let me sink in unclear expectations and nonexistent resources. I remember often wondering why they even hired me. There was no equity in how they positioned me and placed me in my role. Most of my colleagues were white, a couple were Southeast Asian, and all from Ivy League schools. With my non-Ivy League degree and limited experience at the time, I simply did not feel like I fit in there. I was also severely underutilized in terms of my skills.

I remember that while I was working at the consulting firm, I was also in graduate school, and I had to leave at 5 p.m. two or three days a week to attend evening classes, which is something I told my supervisors when I interviewed. But it was clear later on that they felt that this did not make me a team player because I was not staying until 7 p.m. or 8 p.m. eating dinner with the team at the office. For me, this was an equity issue. I was never told that this would be an expectation or requirement of the job. I was willing to come in many hours early in the morning to work and would still stay late when I could, but school was just a top priority for me and my career. Also, I commuted at least an hour by train and bus from home, where I still lived with my mother, which was in an affordable community 25 miles south of Boston. I was also often slighted if I did not meet performance expectations, which frankly were never made clear to me ahead of time. My colleagues were a bunch of elite, college-educated individuals—mostly white but not all—who could afford to live nearby in the city and who were the epitome of white dominant culture in the workplace. They didn't seem to be aware of their privilege. I suppose they told themselves otherwise by ordering Indian food for dinner on late nights and indulging in talking about their international travels and partying with locals. But they were still just spectators of poverty and oppression, and in my opinion, brought a lot of ego to their "charitable" work.

So there I was, sitting across the table from the vice president of the organization, with tears running down my face onto my blazer, feeling like I broke unspoken rule number one—never let them see you cry. The Black female vice president was telling me that they were letting me go. I wondered if because she was a sista' she felt the need to give me some consolation by telling me that I was bright and capable but simply not a "good cultural fit" for that role or company, and that I would be okay. I wondered if they had her do the dirty work because she was a sista. After all, she was one of three bosses, and we were the only two Black people at the company. Needless to say, even though I hated that job, I was devastated. Being fired had validated my imposter syndrome, and I felt like a failure. Was I not smart enough or skilled enough? Was I difficult to work with? Maybe I wasn't a great fit for the role at that time, but rather than mentor me and assess what was not working and why, they just fired me. There were no warnings, no progressive discipline, and no performance improvement plan, and I rarely even had regular supervision. I had never had a professional development or mentoring conversation at that company in my entire 10 months.

I spent a lot of time reflecting after that. I learned that I could survive being fired. I learned from that situation that I needed to have the courage to speak up more and advocate for what I needed to be successful in the workplace. I learned that I never wanted to manage someone the way that I was managed—or rather mismanaged—in that situation. I resolved then to one day be a leader who cared about setting people up for success and making their development a priority, especially when it came to people of color. I also learned that the cultural fit excuse is a total cop out and a trap worth avoiding. More on that later.

Let me tell you about the *second* time I got fired. After working for about seven years at a youth development nonprofit where I truly felt valued, was adequately trained, had access to some meaningful mentoring and coaching, and had meaningful leadership opportunities, I decided I might be ready to move on to learn something new and see what else I could do. I had no vision for my trajectory at that place. I was turning 30 and having a bit of a third life crisis and was ready to move on.

I was hired as an associate director at a regional nonprofit workforce development organization. This was a near executive-level position and resulted in a shiny new title and a 25 percent increase in my pay. I felt that I had arrived. But the morning of my first day I had a terrible anxiety attack while getting ready for work. My stomach was queasy. I figured it was just nerves because I was embarking on something new and was going to be taking on a new level of responsibility. But when I really think back, I felt sick because I had doubts about my cultural fit at that place and if I would fall into the same trap that I had previously. After all, all of the leadership was white—which I was used to, by the way—but so was all of the staff from what I could tell. The leadership was also all over the age of 60. I was just tired of being the "only one" and of what that meant.

I was comforted when I arrived on my first day and was greeted by another new hire who was my age and a sista' with natural hair like me. I would later learn that right before I arrived that morning she had just been berated by our boss, the Executive Director, for having the nerve to decorate her office walls with some temporary stick-on wall decals and placing cultural momentos on her desk and table because she perceived it to be unprofessional. This behavior from my boss toward my coworker ended up being the tone of our entire time at that organization. We each experienced her differently, but what we shared was a firm belief that this woman was bat crazy and a lowkey racist. She often berated us, yelled, and had a dictatorial leadership style. She claimed to want to bring in young, diverse leadership to the team by hiring us and another woman who was Chinese American, but she had no cultural competency, a complete lack of self-awareness and no desire to check her implicit biases. In my opinion, this should be a requirement for managing BIPOC women. The attitudes I described were only directed at us and no one else. Additionally, despite being a woman herself, she was extremely patriarchal in her values. For example, she once told the three of us who were all about 30 years of age and of child-bearing age to be sure not to get pregnant at the same time. She said she didn't want to put resources toward developing more robust 21st-century parental leave policies that include adoption, same-sex parental leave, or maternity leave. She said this in a staff meeting and got away with it.

The patriarchy was one thing, but my boss was also an ageist, often making shady and derogatory comments about our youth and thus lack of experience compared to hers. I once again asked myself, "Why did she hire me then?" The number of microaggressions that I experienced from this woman was untenable. It was so unfortunate because she was actually quite brilliant in so many ways. She was exceptional with numbers and had a very unique technical data analysis skill set for our area of work. She had also basically pioneered the organization and the system in which we worked. But she was a horrible people manager. She was not open to personal feedback, thus was terrible at applying it. She often would have memory lapses, constantly forgetting agreements and directives from our one-to-one meetings. It got to the point where after each meeting I sent follow-up emails with notes to make sure we agreed on next steps and to avoid being accused of not doing my job or misrepresenting the company. She unfortunately saw this as me stepping on her toes. As a matter of fact, any time I managed up or took initiative, she would yell at me, "You're stepping on my toes!" She always yelled except when she would comment on my constantly changing hairstyles and colorful, curve-fitting clothing choices as "interesting" and saying in a condescending tone that she "appreciates versatility." What made it additionally challenging about working there was that there was no Human Resources (HR) team or ombudsman to whom I could complain. It was after this experience that I first thought about making a career shift to HR management.

When I finally had what was to be my first and only annual review, my boss scored me very low. The review was basically a laundry list of what I felt to be her unfounded opinions of my performance and character with no precise data. My evaluation also did not include a 360 review with opinions from others with whom I worked. I did not take it lying down, however. I provided extensive feedback to her about her memory lapses, microaggressions, and inaccuracies in my review, to which she simply replied, "Well, I have to protect *myself* here." The short of it is that was a bad meeting. Afterwards, I went to the bathroom and proceeded to cry in my usual stall. I cried a lot while at that job. It got so bad that I often cried on my hour-and-a-half drive in traffic on the way to work, then cried in the bathroom when I arrived. Sometimes I even went out to my car at lunchtime and cried. Once again, I knew that I had not been set up for success in this role, despite my attempts at self-advocacy and development. I thought to myself, "How am I here again?" Needless to say, my time there was short, and I got fired. Luckily because I knew that this job no longer served me and was negatively affecting my health, I had already been actively pursuing other job opportunities and quickly landed back on my feet. I went on to work for another company in a leadership role for almost seven years. I then left that company after completing my MBA in Human Resources Management because I wanted to make a shift into HR business partnership work focused on diversity, equity, and inclusion and people operations. I am now a co-leader in an executive role at a nonprofit in Cambridge, Massachusetts.

So what did I even learn from all of this? What were my takeaways after years of constant self-reflection and guidance from friends and family?

1. *Avoid the "Cultural Fit" Trap*

It was after my first firing that I first thought about what it really means to be a cultural fit and realized that "cultural fit" thinking is a trap. I think about it like the tourist trap model, which is used in economics to describe the costs incurred as a tourist due to the limited information when buying goods or products in a foreign or unfamiliar land. If you've traveled a bit, you might recognize that tourist traps are often a concentrated grouping of establishments that typically provide services, entertainment, food, souvenirs, and other products for the purpose of making tourists feel good and spend money. Goods become overpriced, and tourists are left exploited due to price uncertainty and a limited budget to cover search costs (e.g., the lack of time they have to find something more cost effective somewhere else). The cultural fit trap exploits people from historically marginalized groups, and we become a spectacle for the employer. They will make us feel like we can be successful if we are willing to only assimilate rather than integrate. We are expected to spend our time and hard work sacrificing who we are to satisfy others and the status quo with limited gains for ourselves. They depend on the idea that if we are given the opportunity, we will just stick with things because the search costs of going somewhere else are uncertain since good opportunities for us seem limited anyway.

Cultural fit tactics in hiring are about making the hiring manager feel good about themselves. They hire someone who is very similar to them in terms of education, socioeconomic status, race, or someone they think will fall in line and not rock the boat. It's a cop out because it does not hold employers accountable for ensuring that all of their employees, regardless of their social identities, have the tools and resources they need to be successful on the job. The cultural fit trap perpetuates bias. With diversity, equity, and inclusion in mind, hiring managers should in fact hire for a cultural add and value add rather than cultural fit.

Here's how you avoid the cultural fit trap. Before applying for a job or entering a new partnership, do your research on that company and their people. See who is in leadership. Use LinkedIn, Facebook, or whatever else you need. Look for any evidence of their values. I no longer apply to jobs for companies that do not have publicly stated values that include something about equity and inclusion and something about work/life balance. This is important to me as a mother and someone prone to anxiety and depression when I don't have time to care for myself properly. When interviewing, I also ask numerous questions to probe about the company's commitment to diversity, equity, and inclusion, their onboarding plan for me if I were hired, what success looks like in the role in the first 90-120 days, and how people spend their time together at work. I ask who is included in decisions and policy-making and who is not. I have also asked about what time people arrive each day and when they leave. I ask if they are ready for someone like me who will disrupt rather than assimilate. These questions can tell you a lot about the values and culture.

2. *Give Yourself Grace to Cry*

It's okay to not be okay sometimes. I used to think that crying because of a job meant that I was weak. But what it means is that I care about doing a great job. It means that I am frustrated and that there is tension in my body that needs to be released. It means that I have been traumatized or harmed. Crying can be cathartic and help us heal. Emotional tears release oxytocin and endorphins that can be soothing. Now, I am not advocating crying in every meeting and letting it flow. If that happens once or twice, excuse yourself, and maybe that's okay. You are human after all. Just know that when you cry, you are allowing yourself to feel your feelings and move toward a path of healing. We carry generations of trauma and daily stress of simply being Black in America in our bodies. In fact, you *should* be crying. James Baldwin said, "To be a Negro in this country and to be relatively conscious is to be in a rage almost all the time." You need a coping mechanism and a way to heal every day. Crying is one way. Physical fitness is also important, and having a routine of self-care is critical to being able to manage these stressors. Most of all, give yourself some grace when you feel like you're falling apart. Tomorrow can be a better day.

3. *You Must Find Your Black Girl Magical North Star*

For me, the paradox of being Black and working in social

justice in the Greater Boston area is that these organizations are designed through the lens of white privilege (the characteristics associated with being white, primarily English speaking, cisgender, male, heterosexual, middle-class or rich, and Christian) that are the very structures that can harm BIPOC workers and the community members. I am constantly trying to figure out how to gain agency for myself in my career and for the communities we serve while also navigating through often covert structures of white dominance and other oppression at those very same institutions that exist to serve marginalized groups while also at times feeling marginalized myself. What gets me through it is, I keep my eye on my north star, my values, and my purpose. I try not to let anything get in the way of that. I feel called to leadership as a Black woman because we need more leaders who look like me in this work. I also strongly value cultural and racial affirmation in the workplace and taking a trauma-informed approach to how I manage people, meaning that I assume they come with some history of trauma and consider the role that may play in how they show up for work on a given day. This is especially critical for women and BIPOC individuals. This is a strong value I hold and what pushes me to have the courage to disrupt processes and structures that I feel do not align with that.

The North Star has been used for navigation for centuries. People have used its brightness in the sky to make certain they are traveling in the right direction. The same applies to how we navigate the workplace as Black women. What I mean by finding your own Black girl magical north star is that you need to know your purpose and your core values when it comes to your work. This concept is used in business as well and is often referred to as a North Star Strategy. My north star also of course includes my five-year-old daughter because I want to help create a better world for her and show her that she can break barriers. I also consider my north star to be disadvantaged youth of color because I feel they are both the promise of the future and the most vulnerable citizens in this country. Sometimes when I am buried in emails or faced with a challenging task, I literally tell myself, "We do it for the kids. We do it to make a change. We do it because it is just." Ask yourself, "What do I want for my life?" Not what others want for you, but what do you want? What are your core values that are non-negotiable in the workplace and at home? What are you willing to do or not do to get there? Ask yourself why. Once you have the answers to these questions written down, keep them with you and check in with them often to make sure you are truly following your north star.

Please always remember that you are filled with magic. Follow your purpose and give yourself some grace. What I learned from my experiences is that I may get knocked down, but I will survive. I also learned that if I keep faith and keep trying, new opportunities will come my way. Each time I was fired, I wondered whether I would get another opportunity like the one I lost. But something better always came along. Like the Black VP sista' told me, I would be okay. You will too.

It's Okay to Pause, But Keep Moving!

WILMA FAYE MATHIS

As an African American woman, I consider it an honor to include my personal experiences in this anthology. I begin my chapter by explaining why I chose to do so. I believe that every person should be treated as a human being and not better or worse depending on the color of their skin. I am voicing my experience of discrimination that stems from structural racism to bring healing into my own life and into the lives of those who read this book. In my recent publication, *An Artistic Tribute to Harriet Tubman*, I define the structural racism, which I describe in this chapter, as:

> "A system in which public policies, institutional practices, cultural representations, and other norms work in various, often reinforcing ways to perpetuate racial group inequity. It identifies dimensions of our history and culture that have allowed privileges associated with "whiteness" and disadvantages associated with "color" to en-

dure and adapt over time. Structural racism is not something that a few people or institutions choose to practice. Instead, it has been a feature of the social, economic, and political systems in which we all exist."[1]

I am contributing my personal experiences to this anthology to stand for racial equity and against the restrictions of structural racism because, for one, I believe in the Scriptures, which do not promote racism, but boldly state, "There is neither Jew nor Gentile, neither slave nor free, nor is there male and female, for you are all one in Christ Jesus" (Galatians 3:28)," for we are all human.[2]

In an October 2020 Brookings Institute Publication, Adia Harvey Wingfield explains: "Women are advancing in the workplace, but women of color are still lagging behind: An oft-cited statistic, for instance, reveals that as a result of factors including, but not limited to, motherhood penalties, gender discrimination, and occupational segregation, women make 79 cents for every dollar men earn. But Black women earn only 64 cents on the dollar, and for Latinas, it is a dismal 54 cents. As it was in the early 20th century, women of color continue to experience occupational and economic disadvantages that reflect the ways both race and gender affect their work experiences."[3]

---

1 "11 Terms You Should Know," lines 1–17.
2 Davis and DeFazio, *An Artistic Tribute to Harriet Tubman*, page 15.
3 Adia Harvey Wingfield, "Women are advancing in the workplace, but women of color are still lagging behind."

Despite these grim statistics of latent structural racism:

"There are black and brown people today who are relentless and have made the conscious decision to fight and not give up: men fighting for a better life, women making sacrifices for their children to ensure they will become a better generation, youth determined not to become a statistic, entrepreneurs with big dreams, little to work with, but taking risks."[4]

I am one of these survivors. Here is my story.

When I think back over my life, I have always been a determined person. Once I get an idea and set my mind on doing something, I will not stop until I've accomplished as much as I am possibly able. The desire to have my independence came at an early age. I started working soon after becoming a teenager. Initially, working was fun. My focus was solely on making money to shop, travel, and do for myself without going to my parents unless it was necessary.

My childhood dream was to be an interior designer or a flight attendant. I did neither, although I still love and dabble in interior design. After junior college, I worked in banking for several years. As an entry-level employee, things were going well. I was later promoted to the position of business analyst. The work was more challenging, but I was always ready to take on new challenges. The role exposed me to other departments, outside vendors, and

---

4   Davis and DeFazio, *An Artistic Tribute to Harriet Tubman*, page 14.

then Informational Technology (IT). The work involved in these areas was very detailed and took a certain degree of analysis. Because I was fascinated with computers, the dynamics of IT was exciting (as it still is today), and I learned how this side of the industry worked. I began to serve as a liaison between the business unit and IT due to my ability to articulate the needs and demands for both. I decided to further my education and pursued a degree in business administration. As my skills sharpened, I was promoted to project specialist. Wow, this was exciting, and I was feeling good about my accomplishments (degree, career, car, and independence). Life was great!

Now, working in a big company, I became familiar with the term "office rumor mill." Coworkers would often say, "it's not everything, but there is some truth to what you hear in the rumor mill, and it would be wise not to dismiss everything." Periodically, I noticed this particular manager lingering around my area. He would appear at my cubicle out of nowhere and say, "Just stopping to say hi." Eventually, that started feeling creepy, and then I remembered the "office rumor mill" term and how this particular manager was, and I quote, "a snake." Anyone who knows me will attest that I do not like and am paranoid of creepy crawlers, especially snakes. I was warned that this manager had a reputation for creeping around looking for whatever he could use against coworkers, particularly women. He would peer over your computer looking for non-work-related activity even though you were on lunch. It got to a point where we would see him creeping up on coworkers while they were talking even though it was their break time. He would use these incidents to call you into his office to address what he noticed. Once this became known, I took the initiative to rearrange my space so my computer monitor did not face the opening of my cubicle, and I would keep my peripheral vision on if I sensed him coming around.

As a project specialist, meetings were part of my job, where I gave updates, project statuses, and next steps. It was exciting to be at this level and be invited to attend meetings with other managers and coworkers. However, there was a downside. I did not always feel comfortable. I would scan the conference room and see there were no other women who resembled me and that males were pre-dominantly present. After the first couple of meetings, I needed to ensure that my presentation was not only good but exceptional. Why did I feel this way? Because whenever I gave my presentation, the room was either silent or just head nods. This was a different response from what some of my counterparts received. Periodically, the manager referred to as "the snake" attended the meetings. He was always critical and found something to disagree with me about, but he was never wrong. At one particular meeting, I felt him staring at me, which was creepy. After I did my presentation, he challenged me on an aspect of my results. For him, it was not complete because I missed things he expected to have been included. Of course, I apologized, said I would review it, and would be sure to include it for next week's meeting.

Before the next meeting, I was called into his office to discuss my presentation. His demeanor and the way he presented himself were unprofessional. What was said in the rumor mill, I saw manifested in his posture: laid back in his office chair, legs crossed on top of the desk, hands behind his neck. So, I sat down, agitated and disrespected. I was raised with a father who exemplified a man, and a respectful one at that. As the manager spoke, his first words were, "You present well but would do better by stating the facts as I told you." I accepted and agreed to do as suggested. Still in the same posture, he said, "I've been here a long while. You're pretty cute, and there can be a future for you here." By this time, I was mad, not only with his posture, but with his subtle advances and how I was being viewed. I immediately dismissed myself from his office giving him "the look" and said, "My presentation will have what you suggested next time" and walked out. I had to pause and regroup for a moment. My first instinct said to go to HR, but I felt there was not enough proof to justify what I encountered. I knew from then on, it would be uneasy passing him in the hallways. Then, one day, while he was with one of his male counterparts, he passed me in the hallway and said, "Black but pretty." Did I also mention that he had clout, talked loudly and abruptly, and was intimidating to people? It was common knowledge that this manager was powerful and rarely confronted. He was involved in illegal matters that finally caught up with him. This later resulted in him no longer being employed at this organization. I was a naïve, young lady at the time, but looking back now, women's inequality existed then, just as it does today.

Jocelyn Frye in her article entitled, "Racism and Sexism Combine to Shortchange Working Black Women" explains:

> "Today, Black women work in a variety of jobs and industries at all different levels. Yet, many Black women still confront the same misperceptions about their work that have formed at the intersection of racial and gender biases for decades. As a result, Black women face unfair expectations, unique challenges, and biased assumptions about where they fit in the workplace that differ from the perceptions held about women from other racial and ethnic groups as well as men."[5]

This experience gave me a different perspective about upper management and what it could cost to move up the ladder. The disrespect for women, the subtle racial bias, and the cut-throat culture had me thinking twice, not because I was incapable, but unwilling to accept disrespect and lower my standards to get ahead. An old proverb says, "The higher you climb, the harder you fall." I witnessed that come true with this manager. Will I continue to climb higher? Absolutely! But not at the cost of lowering my standards.

---

5 Jocelyn Frye, "Racism and Sexism Combine to Shortchange Working Black Women."

I had to keep it moving. My next move, which was a career change, landed me a job in healthcare. This career was rewarding but did not come without challenges. The first few years went well. Reporting to an African-American woman who was all about seeing others advance while she did that for herself was a breath of fresh air. There was an open-door policy, and you felt as if you belonged and were part of a team. After about six years, the biases began to display themselves. My manager worked hard, made accomplishments in the department, and was passed over for a promotion initially intended for her. The disrespect and lack of recognition left her with no recourse but to resign. This left me feeling vulnerable, not knowing where I'd end up. My heart went out for her, and I wished her nothing but the best. Her demonstration of such integrity during the process taught me how to stand up for who I was and to never allow anyone to downplay my worth.

As the years passed, I was fortunate to either have great managers or a level of respect. I tend to think both. However, after several years, I did not receive nor was I offered a promotion. While speaking with management, I had the opportunity to convey my feelings of being overlooked for a promotion. Fortunately, I was heard and later promoted to project manager. In my new role, I had one direct report. I was exposed to various departments, clients, and faculty all while teaching myself different aspects of the healthcare industry that were unfamiliar to me. Eventually, new management was brought in from the outside, and my department was merged and restructured on all levels. It was customary when new management came on board to hold meetings with the existing staff to become familiar with everyone's role.

During my meeting, I conveyed my interests, as I was presented with questions such as:

1. What are your favorite things to work on?

2. What have your previous managers done that you would like me to also do or not do?

3. What are your career goals and where did your last manager leave off with them?

I spent time answering as honestly as I could, confident this manager had my best interest at heart. In short, I communicated that at the time my previous manager left, I was up for a senior promotion with a salary increase. I also knew this was earned and that my accomplishments were reflected in performance appraisals.

Within my department, there was only one other person who resembled me. I started feeling uncomfortable with this new manager because during meetings, I was receiving the cold shoulder. When passing each other in the hallways, there were no greetings, and then I noticed private meetings being held with a select few. I received an invite for a one-on-one meeting. I assumed it was to review what we previously discussed. The afternoon of the meeting, I went into the senior manager's office. The meeting was concerning changes, which was the buzzword at each staff meeting, but it was not what I expected. First, without any detailed conversation, she said, "I've made some changes that I believe you will like" and proceeded to hand me the new organizational chart. To my surprise, two promotions were given—one to a coworker who had been there maybe three years and whom I had trained on my project, in which we were both involved. The senior manager did not address anything we had initially discussed. Hoping it was an oversight, I reiterated that my assigned project was implemented from scratch six years prior. The work invested in this project had not received its full recognition. There were no promotions or salary increases attached, yet I was watching others being promoted. I believed what I was asking for was fair. Disappointed, I said, "You empathized with me and said that you would re-examine the budget, and though there was little wiggle room, I deserved what was promised." The senior manager looked at me and just said, "You will now report to this person listed on the organizational chart" (with emphasis). All I could say—because I wanted to say something different—was, "So it's starting to feel like a situation that goes against what the organization promotes: equal opportunity."

The issue was not with the coworker who was now my direct report. It was with the blatant unfairness, non-recognition for my work, and lack of acknowledgment of what was said would be done on my behalf. I probably would have taken it better if it was at least said, "Wilma, I tried to work with the budget to get what you deserved, and though I'm unable to right now, I will keep trying." There was no apology or empathy. I received more empathy from my coworker when we met a few days later to discuss the next steps on my project. I communicated to my coworker there were no ill feelings on my part. Then she said to me, "I asked senior management, 'Why wasn't this promotion given to Wilma?'" The bias continued to manifest.

By now, the office atmosphere was tense. The senior manager and I had little interaction. I decided to take matters into my own hands and advocate for myself, so I went to HR. Following my conversation with them, I found out several other complaints were received about this senior manager, who eventually resigned. There was some relief, but now what was done was done and could not be reversed. Since every section had a designated HR representative, we were invited to discuss any concerns and how they may be of help. I accepted the invitation, and during the conversation, I recapped my previous discussions with management. Let's just say my best interests were not taken to heart, as I found out later.

Out of nowhere one day, I was approached by the office assistant and told that I should contact the payroll office to have my paycheck switched back to direct deposit. I didn't understand why all of a sudden this was changed but proceeded to payroll to have this researched. While there, a payroll assistant came out and told me that I needed to go downstairs to HR. Once there, I was asked to come into the office and have a seat. I knew something was not right. The HR representative started by telling me "Wilma, we were going to wait until tomorrow, but we might as well do it now" and proceeded to hand me a folder. It was my sep-aration package. In our previous meeting to which I was invited, we spoke about me wanting something different, that I was open to change, and that I would be assisted by HR. So, I was just blind-sided that my position, as they put it, was "being eliminated!" But that was not all. I was told, "Wilma, you remember during our conversation I hinted that you should look for another position." I replied, "You hinted? Absolutely not!" By this time, I had to take another pause moment, otherwise this situation could have gone another way. I was done and had to quickly get out of that office. As I headed back to clear out my office, I decided to visit the Human Relations Officer to find out my legal rights and inform them of all that had taken place. I was advised before signing my separation package that I should let an attorney look it over. It was sad and painful to give an organization so many years of dedication and have it end this way.

Conflict and misunderstandings happen on the job, but to be targeted creates other sorts of emotions because now I was the victim of dirty office politics. I said earli-er this was one of my hesitations with moving into upper management because I cannot and will not be part of the cut-throat culture and the lack of consideration for other human beings. The one other person who resembled me, I later found out, was being disrespected and unappreciated as well. I decided to discuss my situation with an attorney and have them review the separation package. I was curi-ous if this situation fit into the racial bias category. I knew it was evident with my being overlooked, my counterpart being preferred, my yearly merit increase but not receiving a promotion, and advanced training being withheld that racial bias was at play. The attorney agreed with me but stated that the fight would not be worth it and that I would risk losing everything and gaining nothing. This is common, it was stated, that these big corporations know how to camouflage their real intent and job elimination was a way out.

I started thinking of the widespread protest during the 2020 pandemic after George Floyd's murder at the hands of Minneapolis police. The Black Lives Matter movement was fighting for justice for Breonna Taylor, Sandra Bland, Rayshard Brooks, and too many others to name who experienced a harsher standard of treatment by police and the justice system. I then realized that this harsher standard is also present in the workplace. Black and Brown women like me are and have been experiencing this harsher standard while pursuing careers.

My journey is similar to that of many African American women in the workplace. I wrote this chapter for all of us. I have a few takeaways to share from my professional experience.

I grew up hearing "there's a reason for everything" and that "sunshine comes after the storm." I knew I could not stay in my storm and that I needed the sun to shine again. So, I had to find a way to keep moving forward.

These are four things that I learned.

- **Face it:** Look what happened in the face and even allow yourself to grieve. Yes, I said, "grieve." The situation was painful. It left me hurt, sad, and angry. So, it is okay to pause and come to terms with what you want—in my case, the next career path.

- **Trace it:** I was haunted by the idea that maybe I could have fought harder. You have to take an introspective look and realize you need time to heal. I needed to heal from the sting and regret that I did not do more.

- **Erase it:** Keep moving despite fears and the unknown. The time had come for me to "let it go." Apply the lessons that you have learned while coming to terms with what you want in the next stage of your life.

- **Replace it:** Set priorities and have someone to hold you accountable—even if it's your journal. Rediscover your dreams and passions. I created space for some personal projects that were put on hold, addressed health issues that were ignored, and embraced some "me time" that was long overdue. I gave myself space just to be me.

With everything that has happened in the workplace and some other unpleasant situations in my life, my survival has always been rooted in my faith, which simply equates to my complete trust and confidence in my Lord and Savior, Jesus Christ!

My Truth

DANIKA DUKES

My Black sisters, where do I begin? Let me start by acknowledging that the pains of my past have been rooted in silent traumas masked by a smile and shout. Early on in my childhood, I was always told that for a dark-skinned girl, I was beautiful. I always wondered why people thought that was a compliment, because it was not. It made me question the color of my skin and my beauty. I was always seeking validation from others while diminishing my self-esteem. Comments like this left me walking around with my head held down and questioning whether I was enough. These statements were the beginnings of me feeling inadequate.

So you may be wondering, "Okay, how has this impacted who you are now? Let's talk about my childhood. I learned at a very early age that there is nothing abnormal about seeing a child cry. Children cry for various reasons. A simple cry because they are hungry. A cry for attention or just wanting to be held. How I wish those were the reasons for my tears. Unfortunately, my childhood tears were not coming from my tear ducts but from the epitome of my soul. My soul was crying for love and attention from my parents. I was searching for something that was supposed to be normal yet so hard to obtain. Addiction played a role in the lack of attention from my mother and the absence of my father. Everything that was supposed to be the American Dream became my American Cry. Why do I phrase it like that? I will tell you why. As an adolescent, all I heard grown-ups say was, "It takes a village to raise a child." Well, where was my village? I can remember going to school dressed up on the outside and falling apart on the inside, but I "played" the role of a happy little girl because I was told, "What goes on in the house stays in the house."

As children in the Black community, we are taught to believe that you must put up and shut up. That your voice doesn't matter because of statements like "What I say goes" and "You better not talk about what goes on in my house" or "Don't back talk me." These statements have often rang true for many Black families, conditioning us to believe that speaking up is wrong even if what was going on was to the detriment of our wellbeing. Child Protective Services (CPS) was a very prominent factor back in my day. I quickly learned that opening up to the wrong person could cause big conflict in my home and could even result in being taken from the abnormal American Dream. I wanted and needed for someone to hear my cry and look beyond my smile.

At the age of ten, I found myself indulging in a greater power that gave me such peace and tranquility. I would go to church, crying out to the one who eased my pain. The one to whom I gave my all when no one else understood my shouting the pain away. Praising the pain away and crying the pain away. Church was my outlet. Every time that the doors were open, I was there. It was a safe haven as well as an opportunity to have positive socialization with other young folks. Whether they wanted to be there or were forced to be there was another thing. I just know it was my saving grace. I was there to get a release. To unload. I had such an encounter with God that I knew this would be a forever thing. I found a peace that I wanted to hold on to. God was with me in spirit, easing my pain, giving me strength to endure at such a young age.

As I got older, masking my hurt became a thing for me. I acted as if I was okay. Addiction played a major role in my family, so I don't blame them for not being attentive to my needs. When you are addicted to something, that thing has total control over your wellbeing and your state of mind. My only wish was that when my loved ones came to a sober mindset, they would see and realize the damage they were causing. But because we had a roof over our head, clothes on our back, and food on our table, everything was okay. It didn't matter. My brother was so strong, he was able to maintain normalcy while living in chaos. I often wondered how he did it. He kept a social life, he worked, and he had friends with whom he spent time, all while maintaining his peace. So why was it hard for me? I expected more from my family, and they could only give me the capacity of nurturing that their occasional sober minds allowed them to.

I quickly learned to stop focusing on them and tried to obtain whatever happiness I possibly could.

I was trying so hard to be accepted, but I was only being shown fake love by all the people I thought loved me. I was babysitting for people I thought cared about me for hours at a time, only to receive fifteen dollars. What I realized is that half the time I only said yes because it gave me a different environment to be in despite being used and taken advantage of. I did everything to be accepted and to keep the peace because I didn't want to lose the little bit of solace that I had. I was still bleeding on the inside and smiling on the outside because I didn't want to speak up or create any issues, problems, or discomfort for myself or others. My voice was silenced from all the traumas of a young girl. As I began to grow and develop, I became more and more timid and didn't speak up for myself. People often say "closed mouths don't get fed." My mouth was not closed due to the lack of nourishment, but due to the lack of affirmation, confidence, and self-esteem. I gave people the power to manipulate me and control me because I lost my voice. My teenage and young adult years only got worse, allowing boys and men to break my heart just because I was looking for love in all the wrong places. Mentally and emotionally, I was tired, but my heart was looking for love. The abuse at the time didn't bother me, because these men were giving me more than I was getting at home. I often asked myself why I allowed myself to be treated in such a manner. I didn't know any better, but I wanted better. I wanted more, but I didn't know how to obtain it. I was never taught or shown what love was or what it looked like or how I was supposed to be treated. So I accepted what was given to me. Heartbreak after heartbreak.

As time passed, I felt my life trying to gain stability. I was working and going to school at night, and I wasn't so fragile. I ended up in night school due to all the bad decisions and choices I had made growing up. I couldn't focus in day school looking at all my friends so happy and living normal lives while I was struggling. My grades were horrible because I was not focused. The only thing that got me through was being the class clown making everyone laugh, although deep down inside, I was bleeding. Deciding to quit school was hard because my uncle once told me that I was going to be a statistic. A young Black girl in the system with a baby. I didn't want that for my life. I was fighting hard to become a better me. Getting pregnant at 16 and having a miscarriage was quite the experience, but I knew God had a plan for my life. I just had to fight. There were many times I grew weary, but I knew that I could not give up on myself.

I was still in church giving God all the praise for keeping my mind and heart in perfect peace in spite of all the childhood trauma. I graduated from night school and received my high school diploma. I was working, and I was proud of myself. I had to change my perspective even though some of the things around me did not change. I no longer wanted to drown in my own tears. I had the choice to sink or swim, and I decided to swim. I had to create the voice that was taken from me, and at this point and junction in my life I was ready to be heard. Just because I was ready to be heard does not mean that there were not times in my life when I was either silent or silenced. I was given the opportunity to live on my own, and I took it. Another issue resolved in my life was not having to dumb down to anyone just to have a roof over my head.

At the age of twenty-one, I became pregnant with my first child. I was excited because I knew this was going to be a reciprocal love. My mother ended up going to rehab, and I was so proud of her. Her soul was tired, and I could tell. She needed a place to stay, so she moved in with me. I never really received an apology from her, but I knew she was sorry because she showed it in her acts of service. She made sure every morning before I went to work that I had a full breakfast and that when I returned home there was a full-course meal waiting. She made sure everything in the house was clean, and I appreciated her for that. My mother was beautiful, and when she was clean and sober, I looked at her so differently from how I used to. There were some health challenges that she faced, but she persevered.

For a while, it felt like life was going well! My mother was working. I was working and still pregnant, but we had a routine that worked for us. One night, our world was shaken with the unthinkable. My mother received a phone call that my brother had passed away, and that shook her to the very core. I can remember trying to get home to get to my mother and grandmother. When I walked in the house, my mother was crying and smoking a cigarette. I started to cry, and I said, "Please, Debbie, don't smoke." I called my mom by her name. I said that because she had not smoked in a long time, and I knew what would come next—a greater high to ease the pain. I felt so bad for my mother. She had just started to put her life back together, and now to lose her eldest child was devastating. She loved both of us deeply, but I believe my brother was her love child because he stuck by her through the high and lows of her life. My brother and my mother were in a major car accident before he passed, and after the accident, he started to have seizures. They were very controllable at times, but this time it was not. I loved my brother. He meant the world to me. To see him persevere in the midst of pressure made me look up to him.

The day came to bury my brother, and there was not one seat in the church available. In fact, it was a standing room only. Unfortunately, my grandmother was not there to say her last goodbyes to my brother because she was admitted in the hospital. I believe it was due to stress and the fact that she had just lost her eldest grandson. My father was a wreck. He could hardly pull himself together. It was a sad day for our family. We lost a gentle giant who always brought a smile to the table no matter what was being served. When the funeral was over, my mother literally grabbed the casket and just sobbed uncontrollably. I had no words. I was so numb knowing that my little girl would never get to meet her uncle. All of a sudden, the thought just hit me. I said to myself I would miss her like crazy, but my mother had to leave Massachusetts. I said that because I did not want my mother to go backwards. She had come too far. The reality was I think my mother knew that too. I didn't even know it, but she asked my aunt if she could go back to Virginia with her. After the repass, all my family got back on the road to go home, taking my mother with them. I was hurt. I felt like she left me again, but this time she left to save her life. I knew that if my mother stayed in Massachusetts, it would lead to her death.

Eventually my grandmother came home from the hospital and was doing well. She became my best friend. I could lean and depend on my grandmother for anything. There were times I didn't want to be alone at home, so I would just stay over at her house. When I had my cravings, I would tell her, and she made sure that when I came home from work it was hot and ready. She was my sounding board when things didn't make sense to me. When my mother moved to Virginia, I asked my grandmother to be in the delivery room with me. She said, "Yes, absolutely." I knew there were times that my grandmother lost her voice seeing her grown children suffer from addiction or being incarcerated. I know it made her question herself as to where she went wrong as a mother, sometimes even engaging in the activities herself and not having the will to speak up as the mother. I believe that's why she went so hard for her grandchildren, making sure we had what we needed and trying to fill the voids, all while masking her own pain.

After my brother passed, my father tried to build a relationship with me, but I was being stubborn. I thought about some of the things I went through because of him being an absent father and would resist the chance to build a true relationship with him, hardened by the pain I felt he had caused in my life. He was not there when I needed him the most, which left me vulnerable to boys and men and looking for love in all the wrong places. Not knowing my worth left me with no voice and a bunch of empty promises.

As time went on, I felt like masking my feelings and pain had become a part of my life again. I felt that I had to hide my feelings and concerns just to appease the feelings of someone else. I was tired of living like that. It was draining, and I felt like I was abusing myself. Anger, bitterness, frustration, and resentment began to set in. I didn't want to feel this way, but I was faced with so much opposition. People whom I thought were in my corner were never really there. They were actually sitting back watching to see if I was going to fail. I rose to the occasion each and every time. I was determined to persevere and beat the odds that were stacked against me.

The day came to give birth to my baby girl. I was excited and nervous. I was ready to be a mother and ready to pour all this love and attention into someone whom I knew was going to love me for me. Someone with whom I could be vulnerable through trial and error with no judgment. My daughter and I already had one thing in common—we both had absent fathers. But I was willing to give my daughter all of me. I remember being rushed to the hospital and being admitted and ready to give birth. My daughter's godmother and my grandmother were in the room with me. That pain was excruciating, but it was worth it to see my beautiful baby girl enter this world. My grandmother was so happy. The look on her face was priceless. She never left my side. My grandmother was a blessing to me. She just stepped up and took her rightful place as a great grandmother.

Over the next several years, I experienced multiple losses of my mother, father, and grandmother. I buried my parents literally a week apart. I left one state to go to the next state to grieve all over again. What a cliché! Having such great losses in my life had a direct impact on my emotional development. It impacted my ability to nurture, give love, and receive love. I also suffered from separation anxiety, never allowing anyone to get too close to me, nor did I allow myself to become too attached. I was always ready to disappear, which caused me to build a defense mechanism—fight or flight. But honestly speaking, most of the time I never really fought. I would just disappear. It had become so easy to be confined to my own world, not having to deal with what was going on on the outside of my four walls or having to deal with any issues. The four walls allowed me to be at peace with what I was dealing with, not having to mask my feelings, part my lips to smile, or give the notion that I was okay. I was able to have a pity party and sulk. Did that help? No. It made matters worse. The depression heightened, and the masking became even greater. It is vitally important to seek help when dealing with grief or anything in your life that is traumatic. Reach out to someone who can help sort out your feelings or simply help you to process grief and trauma.

I made a promise to myself that I was going to teach my daughter how to love herself, value herself, and know her worth. I'm going to let her know it's okay to not mask her feelings, to always speak up for herself, and to never decrease who she is in order to increase someone else. I also decided that I would never use the statement "What goes on in my house stays in my house." I never want her to feel like if her life is in jeopardy that she can't seek help. I want her to know that having confidence in who she is is not a bad thing but to always be humble. I will teach her to take her world by force and to be in control of her feelings and any hardship that she faces. To always work hard for anything she wants in life, because in this life, nobody is going to hand her anything. To make sure every deposit is made with love and affirmation so she does not look for love in all the wrong places. To always stand tall in her true self.

Losing my family left me yearning for a family to call my own. I was longing for this void to be filled, but in the meantime, joining other families for holidays or special events is what I did until God blessed me with my own. Even though I knew they cared for my daughter and me, it just was not the same. Going home after the festivities was so lonely, but I quickly learned not to focus on what I didn't have but instead on what I did have, and that was a beautiful baby girl who needed her mother to be happy and whole.

After years of heartache and sadness, I met a man who made me happy and eventually became my husband. Our wedding was bittersweet because I didn't have my father to walk me down the aisle or my mother sitting in the front row. But what I did have were some very close family members and friends who were in full support of my special day. I felt whole. I felt complete. I had someone to love my daughter and me like their own. A family with whom to bond and share holidays. I thought I knew what it was to be a wife. I had the domestic area down pat. I knew how to take care of children because I had done that all my life. I could cook a meal. I thought I was all set. What I did not know was that the fragment of my broken pieces would surface in my marriage. I had not seen a grief counselor or anyone to help me cope with the losses, so many different feelings and emotions began to surface. I did not know how to deal with conflict or show enough affection. My husband's love language was physical touch. Mine was acts of service because growing up, as long as the essentials were provided, then you had everything you needed. You were okay. So you didn't look for a hug or any affection because it was a generational curse that had trickled down from my great-grandparents, and no one ever knew what was actually taking place. Pure, genuine love and affection were lacking. Simple things like being tucked in at night, being read a bedtime story, or even being told "I love you" on a daily basis did not happen in my household. I didn't even have anyone to model after when it came to marriage because no one in my immediate family was ever married except for my grandmother, but I was not born during that era. She even ended up separating from her husband and moving away. So I never had any role models for marriage.

The little things matter, because if you don't deal with the little things, when you become an adult they become big things. So the issues that you thought you were over or healed from are only issues that have become suppressed because you didn't deal with them. It's important for your voice to be heard. Someone needs you to be you and unapologetically you. I had to learn that.

Some might ask why I am telling my family's business. It's because someone needs to hear there is life after trauma and death. Someone needs to hear that even in their addiction and shortcomings, God still has a plan for their life. There is someone out there waiting to hear how you survived your cry and how you made it through your valley. So roar loud, lioness. There is a den full of other lionesses waiting for you to take the reins.

So I say all of this to say Black girls cry!

From Powerless
to Powerful

***

DRETONA T. MADDOX

My maternal family, including my grandmother, was born and raised in Indianola, Mississippi, commonly referred to as the Mississippi Delta. My grandmother had an eighth-grade education and worked in the cotton fields as a sharecropper. She harvested cotton with her hands until they bled and taught her six children to do the same. When the cotton-picking season was over, my grandmother and her older children would travel to Florida on the back of a truck to work as maids. When the cotton season began again, she and her children would travel back to the Mississippi Delta to prepare for the harvesting season. My grandmother would often say that Jim Crow laws governed her interactions with white people and that she was never really "free." My grandmother had hopes of one day completing her high school education and obtaining her college degree. She talked about having goals and dreamed of living a life where she did not have to keep her head down when approaching white people. So it's no surprise that in the early 1970s, when given a chance to leave

Mississippi and come to California, my grandmother took a leap of faith and headed West to the Golden State with her three youngest daughters, her sister, and her niece. She viewed California as a ticket to freedom and opportunity to advance.

I grew up in the South Central region of Los Angeles, California. This neighborhood was commonly known as "South Central LA" or "the hood." On the weekends, the guys played street football, and the girls played double-dutch in the front yards and giggled at the attention they received from the fellows. Grandmothers sat on their porches, monitoring and censoring the communication between the young girls and boys in the neighborhood. They commonly referred to the young ladies as "fast-tailed gals" or "womanish" and the young men as "manish" or "smelling his own britches." They would often yell at their grandchildren's behavior while blaming their offspring for leaving them with the responsibility of rearing yet another generation of children. In the 1970s and 1980s, grandmothers were the staples of the Black community. They served as the community's gatekeepers, knowing and spreading all the neighborhood's gossip. They shared whispers and stories of tragedy as they navigated their way back to empty nesters, or at least they would hope.

In those days, it was common for grandparents to rear their grandchildren. The substance abuse crisis had wreaked havoc on Black families, causing grandparents to step up and step in as primary caretakers of their grandchildren. This was the case on our street in the heart of

South Central LA. Our neighborhood consisted of grand-mothers but no grandfathers. There were also dope deal-ers, substance users and abusers, gangbangers, a Baptist church, and a liquor store on the corner directly across the street from the church. The entire population of my com-munity was Black.

I was four years old when I moved into "the hood." At the age of 26, my mother died of a suicide-related drug overdose. My grandmother reluctantly became the guard-ian of me and my siblings. She was forty-nine years old when my mother died, and she resented the fact that my mother had taken her own life. She was angry about having to start over with raising small children again. At the time, I didn't understand her frustration. I often wondered why she had accepted the responsibility of being a parent again if she would be so angry all of the time.

After my mother died, my grandmother moved from her one-bedroom house and rented a large enough prop-erty to house three additional children. My sister, who was nine at the time of my mother's death, was diagnosed at birth with cerebral palsy, so my grandmother had to con-sider her unique needs. Cerebral palsy is a movement dis-order that affected my sister's ability to walk and talk. She was also not able to control her movement, balance, and posture. My sister required a wheelchair and other adap-tive equipment to assist with activities of daily living. With all that there was to consider, fortunately, my grandmother was able to find a house in South Central LA. This neigh-borhood became the foundation for learning my culture.

All the kids in my neighborhood attended the same elementary school. Our elementary, junior high, and high school were walking distance, within a two to five miles radius of our home. It was beneficial for community members to live near the schools because most of our caretakers did not drive. We walked and used public transportation to shop for groceries and to pay bills. All of the students who attended our schools were Black and Brown. The majority of our teachers were also Black and Brown. I saw my reflection every day, and I thrived in an environment that nurtured our culture and understood our history, victories, traumas, and complexities. We had a strong sense of community and belonging. I attended the same elementary school from kindergarten until sixth grade. After my sixth-grade graduation, in the summer of 1985, my life was utterly changed *again*.

Every year, our elementary school would have assemblies. They would serve as celebrations of academic achievement, school performances, and information sessions. On this particular occasion, our school was preparing for our sixth-grade graduation. We were practicing our graduation songs and speeches, learning how to march in, and receiving our seating assignments. There was a sense of excitement for the future as we prepared to transition from elementary to junior high school. We had become the most popular kids as graduates, and we scoffed at the thought of being "scrubs" as incoming students. You could feel anticipation and excitement as we giggled and laughed as we were about to embark upon this new venture. We heard horror stories about being thrown in trash cans as a part of our junior high initiation. There was such anticipation in the air. As the assembly started, the chatter slowed and then stopped as curiosity and a little bit of fear filled the room. We had guests—a few white men dressed in suits. Our principal began to speak and say words like school de-segregation, integration, bussing, San Fernando Valley, and opportunity. There was a buzz in the room from the students' confusion, and our teachers told the students to be quiet and listen. I remember the feeling of my heart beating fast. My breaths were also rapid. I could not believe what I was hearing.

I felt betrayed by our school's faculty as they nodded in agreement and shared expressions of gratitude. As the assembly ended, the teachers handed the students a pamphlet to take home to their parents. Although I was disappointed in the faculty, I left the auditorium with the inner peace of knowing that my grandmother would *never* allow me to get bussed out of our neighborhood to integrate into a predominantly white community. I was wrong.

My grandmother had already begun conversations with the school's faculty. She decided on what she and the others believed was best for me. I was given no choice in my educational plan. And to make matters worse, I was told that my childhood best friend would remain in our community and attend the local junior high school. I was so devastated by these findings that I spent days crying in my room underneath my wooden elevated platform bed in a space that I had carved out as my sacred space.

My bed had two drawers in the middle of the front side with areas for books on each side of the drawers. The design of the bed left a hollow space underneath the backside of the bed that was positioned against the wall. In this space, I made a palate with a comforter, sheets, and pillows. I decorated my sacred space with my favorite colors: navy blue, gold, and tan. I sprayed perfume on the pillows and my teddy bears and used dryer sheets to ensure that the fragrance lingered. It was in this space that I found peace and comfort. It was in this sacred space that I could drown out the noise, read books, and dream about my future.

I had the entire summer of 1985 to get adjusted to the idea of waking up at 5:30 am on school days, walking to a bus stop in the dark, and leaving my community to attend a predominantly white school in a mostly white neighborhood without my best friend. My grandmother had given me three hundred dollars—one hundred dollars during each of the summer months—to purchase new school clothes. My friends and I were excited to go school shopping at the local swap meet, the Alley, and the Cooper Building in downtown Los Angeles. Our shopping list included five pairs of pants, seven shirts, two pairs of shoes, socks, panties, two bras, a belt, a backpack, paper, pens, and pencils with a sharpener.

I was twelve years old on the first day of junior high school. I remember preparing for the first day of school as if I was yesterday. In our household, we were only allowed to take full baths on Saturdays. On the other days of the week, we had to take sink baths or "wash-ups." However, because the next day was the first day at the new school, my grandmother allowed my siblings and me to take a bath on a Sunday. I found this allowance to be so unusual because she considered Sundays "The Lord's Day," and we were not allowed to do anything pertaining to the flesh except for eating and going to church. I asked myself if she would have made this exception if we were going to a school in our neighborhood. I could hardly sleep that night. I had racing thoughts about how I would be treated. However, lost in my thoughts, I fell asleep and was awakened after what seemed like only ten minutes to my grandmother screaming my name and telling me to get up and get dressed before I missed my school bus. I understood her concern because she did not drive, and if I missed the bus, I would miss a day of school. At the sound of her voice, I jumped out of bed, running to the bathroom to start my morning preparation for school.

The bus stop was approximately two miles from our home. When I arrived, I recognized some of the neighborhood kids from my elementary school, but not anyone from my block. It was still dark outside, and I could feel the nervous jitters in my stomach. Multiple buses were arriving at the bus stop. With anticipation, I anxiously searched for my assigned bus. Once boarded, I quickly found a seat next to the window. I did not talk to anyone, and I stared out the window the entire ride to school. Our bus made several stops, picking up children all over Los Angeles County before making our way to the school campuses. By the time we arrived at the school, the sun had already come up. The feelings of fear overwhelmed me as the students un-boarded the bus and were met by an aggregate of all white teachers and staff.

Returning students gathered in small huddles at varying distances from the breakfast tables and stared at us Black students picking up our breakfast and sitting down to eat. Some students greeted us with warm but nervous "hello." I was not interested in making new friends, so I quickly ate my breakfast and began my uphill journey to pick up my class schedule and find my classes. I finally made it to my homeroom class and sat down at my assigned seat. After the roll call, the teacher began her welcome speech. But what she said in her welcome address would awaken a determination that persisted throughout my life. She was going over the grading system, and she mentioned that because we were coming in from the inner-city schools, if we received a C on our report card, consider it an A. Wait, what?

Inner-city schools in the Black community were considered underserved and inadequate. Yet, instead of putting forth the effort and money to improve those deficiencies and inefficiencies, parents were made to believe that integrating into schools populated mainly by white students would give Black students a better education. The computers and books may have been in better shape, but I learned who I was as a Black person in America in the Black community. I thrived in a community that looked like me and that demonstrated strength and resiliency. Affected by my homeroom teacher's statement, I purposed in my mind to prove to her and her colleagues wrong. As the days went on, getting good grades would be the least of my worries.

It did not take me long to get adjusted to the new school and the travel arrangements. Getting up at the crack of dawn and making it to the bus stop on time became routine in a relatively short time. I quickly got adjusted to having six different classes. The faculty and students were not all friendly, but not mean either. After a few months, I still had not developed friendships at the new school. Although I did not let it bother me, I did wonder about it. Now, I cannot confidently say that the experience I am about to share is directly related to why no one befriended me, but it would lend to my biases toward my white peers.

Physical education (PE) was one of my best classes of the day. I loved physical exercise, and I loved being outdoors. There was something about running in the fresh air that caused me to feel unstoppable. One day while changing into my PE clothes in the locker room, a white female student standing with her friends pointed at me and called me a "nigger." This group of about four girls immediately started laughing. I asked her if she was talking about me, and she just repeated the derogatory term. I was utterly shocked. I had never been called this term, and I had difficulty understanding why she referred to me in that way. I only had contact with her in PE class, and even then, we did speak to each other. I demanded that she not address me that way, yet she persisted. The verbal attack with racial slurs continued for over a week before I told my grandmother. Once I told her, she instructed me not to say anything to the student and not report the incidents to the teacher because she did not want any school problems. "Any school problem?!" I experienced racism, yet she did not want me to defend myself or report to the proper authorities. I felt unprotected, unsafe, confused, and angry. I knew that I would have to advocate for myself because my grandmother was paralyzed with fear about the possible outcome.

My grandmother had lived experiences with racism while living in Mississippi. She often told stories about the details of how Emmett Till was lynched and brutally murdered in a town near where she was born and raised and had raised her children. She communicated her fear through her unspoken words and expressions. Even so, I was determined not to allow her fears to overtake me. I did nothing wrong, and if I was a target because I was Black, then people who felt that way would have to say it to my face. The next day, I reported the student to my PE teacher, and she told me to ignore the student. I could not believe what I was hearing. I insisted that I had ignored her and that she continued to attack me with racial slurs. My teacher stopped talking and did not instruct me any further. After PE class that day, I walked past this student as she was sitting on the bench bent forward, taking some items out of her lower locker. As I approached this student, I drew my leg back and kicked forward toward her locker with a slight jump. The locker slammed closed with her finger in it. She started to scream, and I ran to my next class. Within a short period, my name was called over the intercom system. "Dretona Moore, please report to the office." This statement was repeated several times, and I could sense the urgency in the announcer's voice. I was expelled from the school and transferred to another school in San Fernando Valley. I do not promote or condone violence. However, learning to advocate for yourself constructively will help prevent physical violence due to powerlessness.

I often think about how I could have handled this student's verbal attacks with racial slurs differently. In retrospect, I realized that I needed a tribe to support me as I navigated through this new community. While at this school, I did not have friends, but I also never showed myself as friendly. I was so focused on academic performance that I failed to build a peer support system. It did not take me long to figure out what I lacked once I got transferred to a new school. I no longer isolated myself and opened up to find a group to build a sub-community or tribe.

I spent the next two and a half years at the new junior high school. I flourished as I met new friends and accepted my new normal. I could not change my circumstances, but I could change my behavior and attitude. In all honesty, the school's environment was good for me. I learned about different cultures and was exposed to a whole world outside of South Central Los Angeles. The students from the inner-city became co-learners with the students, teachers, and staff from the valley.

The truth is that being a Black girl in a white space is scary. But God allowed my experiences with bussing to reveal that I feared the unknown and doubted my ability to perform in a foreign environment. At the same time, I learned that fear and self-doubt are two things that every normal person faces. These are also two of the biggest obstacles to success and happiness. You see, although I did not have physical parents, God was my teacher. Where others had failed to protect, God was using those experiences to teach me at a young age to 1) create a sacred space for myself, 2) seek to know my worth, 3) be my own advocate, 4) find my tribe, and 5) trust the process. Sometimes I sit and marvel at the intentionality of God's plan for man. He positioned me for purpose and took me on a journey to discover His intention for my life. Today, I take bold action. I laugh in the face of fear and make my mark on the world. I show the world just how powerful and fearless a person can be.

How Dare You Not Be Great?

HEIDI LEWIS

"Our deepest fear is that we are powerful beyond measure."
—Marianne Williamson

I never wondered where my strong will and determination to survive came from. It's my inheritance. I grew up in a family of women who had experienced the hardships of life, teenage pregnancy, death of husbands and children, and rumors of infidelity, and they survived. These women instilled in me and my cousins a sense of pride and a spirit of excellence. They taught us that we could be and do anything. Growing up in this environment meant there were certain expectations. Whether real or perceived, they were there. We were expected to do well in school, to do everything with excellence, and to never half step. I lived with the sense that I needed to make them proud. In doing so, I learned to mask, or as I call it, "hide in plain sight." In other words, I showed up as someone that I wasn't. I didn't understand the richness of my inheritance, who I was, and the value of what being me brought to the world.

My grandmother Mary reigned over the family with her own brand of wisdom and strength. At five feet tall with caramel skin, long black hair, and a coke bottle figure, she was both beautiful and formidable. Like her mother before her, who was forced to leave her firstborn child in the care of others, Nana was the type of woman who, through every obstacle or challenge life presented, was able to pay the bills, put food on the table, and keep her girls clothed. I recall being told of the many sacrifices she made and about how she would go to work in the winter with no stockings on so her girls would have lunch money. Nana would go into the high-end department stores and look through the racks of dresses and go home and create patterns out of newspaper to make the same dresses she saw in the stores. I was also told of the time when my mother needed two dresses for her eighth-grade graduation—one for the ceremony and one for the after-party. With no money, somehow my grandmother made it happen.

Nana believed in appearances and making sure everything was done properly. Nothing was ever as it appeared. I think she had every Emily Post book. She taught us how to set a table, what each fork, knife, and spoon were used for, and how to tell the difference between a teaspoon and a jam spoon. This sense of pride and belief that we could be or do anything caused us to hold our heads higher. My family was often accused by others of being uppity or thinking of ourselves more highly than we ought to have. For Nana and for us, it was part of being the best we could be.

My parents left Plainfield, New Jersey when I was two years old and moved to Boston. Within two years, my mother was widowed at 29 years old, left behind with three young children. She didn't know anything about the bills. She knew how to cook and clean and to take care of me and my siblings. She knew bills needed to be paid, but had no idea how to pay them. My father took care of everything. He was a great provider, and we wanted for nothing. After he passed away, our standard of living changed. There were no more brand-new cars or fancy clothes or bedrooms with arcade-sized pinball machines. There were no more beautiful apartments with gleaming hardwood floors and giant picturesque windows. I remember our electricity being shut off. In order to keep the refrigerator running so food wouldn't spoil, Mom ran an extension cord from our apartment across the back porch to our neighbor's apartment next door. Nana taught Mom how to pay the bills. She told her to call all the bill collectors and make a plan to pay them. Without my father's income, Mom wasn't able to afford the apartment we lived in. She had no choice but to move us into the projects. We left a tree-lined street with houses with front porches decorated with flower boxes and swings and moved into a small three-bedroom apartment where I shared a room with my two sisters. By the time I was teenager, I ended up sleeping on the pullout couch in the living room. If there was company, I had to sleep in my mom's room until they went home. I hated visiting family who still lived in our old neighborhood. I pretended that our new neighborhood was great. I bragged about the playground even though we weren't allowed to go there. The projects always seemed dark and dingy. The buildings somehow hid the sunlight. Mom bought window boxes one spring and planted all sorts of flowers that bloomed well into the fall. It reminded me of the play *A Raisin in the Sun* with the small plant on the windowsill. Like Mama Lena in *A Raisin in the Sun*, my mother took special care of the flowers in her window boxes.

Despite all these major life changes, I still believed that I could be and do anything. Remember I said we were accused of being uppity? Well, this belief system didn't go over very well living in the projects when people were struggling with generational poverty and oppression. My mother was used to a middle-class lifestyle. While our current circumstance wasn't middle class, we had a middle-class mindset. This made us different, and that difference made us the target of bullies. We were teased for speaking the "Queen's English." We were asked, "Why y'all tryna' sound white?" or told "Y'all talk like white people." Interestingly, classism existed even in the projects. My sister was bullied because of her dark skin. They would sing the Big Jim Broonzy song lyrics, "If you're white you're alright, if you're brown stick around, if you're black get back." They didn't know the song protested preferential treatment based on skin color. What's more, with the exception of a few Puerto Rican or Cuban families, everyone in the Projects, or "the P," was Black. I was told I was ugly and called four eyes because I wore glasses. We inherited my grandmother's long hair, which Mom used to comb into two high pony-tails that hung past our shoulders. We were told we thought we were better than everyone else because of our long hair. We were taunted because we didn't wear converse sneakers or because we wore hand-me-downs, even though very few families could afford converses. The grown women talked about my mother because she had a 22-inch waist and long hair and walked like Bette Davis. "Hmph. I don't know who she thinks she is, all high sidity."

I had very few friends. I learned that I had to fight (literally) for everything. The bullying caused me to be ex-tremely introverted. I tried to be invisible. I held my head down hoping no one could see me. I didn't speak much, especially to those who didn't live in my immediate section of the projects. I did everything I could so as not to bring attention to myself. I was afraid all the time that someone would notice me and start calling me names or chase me home from school. How on earth did I for one moment believe I could be and do anything when I lived in fear? However, no one ever knew I was afraid. I learned to hide that too. I was taught something else: "Never let them see you sweat."

My greatest joy was walking to James Michael Curley Elementary School, where I discovered my love for reading and poetry. I can still recite *Stopping by the Woods on a Snowy Evening* by Robert Frost. I adored my teacher Mrs. Moorehouse. I was one of the best students in class, win-ning the honor roll and school spirit awards. But of course,

I was bullied for being the teacher's pet and a bookworm. When my so-called friends rejected me, I'd spend my time reading and writing stories and watching old black-and-white movies on TV or football on Sundays. They were my escape from the world around me. Mom would force me out of my solitary world and make me go out to play.

Education was a priority because none of the women in my family graduated high school, not because they weren't smart, but because life got in the way. Both of my aunts were teenage mothers, and my own mom married at seventeen years old. I'm not sure when I realized it, but somehow, I think I always knew I'd be the first in my family to graduate high school and go off to college. Like many of you, I carried the hopes and dreams of my family.

By middle school, I was being bussed along with all the other inner-city kids to schools outside of our neighborhood. These were probably the worst years of my entire life. Not only was the bullying constant by kids from my own neighborhood, but now from those from other neighborhoods too. So once again, I became invisible. I withdrew further into myself. My only friend in school was a white girl whom I'll call Debbie. We sat next to each other in class, spent time together during lunch, and even talked on the phone every night. The girls from the neighborhood were jealous of Debbie because she was full breasted. The boys loved her. One day, a rumor got started that she wasn't wearing a bra. Instead of coming to her defense, I said nothing. I didn't sit with her at lunch that day. When she called me that evening, she asked me why I was acting funny toward her. I told her about the rumor. She said she came to school with no bra because she had no clean clothes. She really told me off for going along with the crowd and said she didn't want to be my friend anymore. I was devastated. How could I tell her that I didn't know how to defend myself? I certainly couldn't defend her. How could I make her understand that I believed I had no other choice but to go along with the crowd?

Amid all of this, I was exposed to racism for the first time in my life. The teachers treated the inner-city kids as if we were stupid. I had to prove that I was smart and that I could more than hold my own. As eighth grade graduation approached, I began thinking about high school. The thought of spending another four years with these people was too much for me. You see, it was a known fact that the majority of us would attend Brighton High. Oh God! I just couldn't do it. But then one of the older guys in my neighborhood suggested I sign up to attend Boston English High. So, when the ballot arrived in the mail, English was my first choice. I got in. I had already planned to quit school if I hadn't.

I blossomed in high school. I was popular. I was all the things I'd never been before. I no longer tried to be invisible. Or so I thought. This time, my hiding showed up as needing to fit in. I had a job and no longer wore hand-me downs. I spent my money on clothes and shoes and became known as one of the best dressed. Freshman year was great. I made real friends and never again depended on those people from "the P" for validation. They laughed because English High didn't provide school buses for us and they talked about how I thought I was better than them because I went to the "Big E" (English High was a 10-story tower with a huge plaza and escalators). I didn't care anymore. So what?

I started cutting classes and was hanging out in the fifth-floor ladies room playing Pitty Pat and smoking cigarettes. My grades were horrible. I ran with a tough crowd that included several of my cousins. Our names came up every time something went down. I'll never forget the day Mom kept me home from school to run an errand with her. Unbeknownst to me, there was a big brawl in school that day, and all of my friends were suspended. The next day as I entered the building, I was pulled aside by a plain-clothed security guard, or what we call a "floor walker." I was asked, "Why are you here? You're on suspension." What?! I had to prove that I wasn't in school the day before. Let me tell you, I was in so much trouble at home. Mom found out about my bad grades. I was on punishment for what felt like a lifetime. I learned to balance hanging out with my friends and going to class. I would still play Pitty Pat and smoke cigarettes, but I also got my work done.

The closer I got to graduation, the harder it was to live up to all of the expectations. My life had been mapped out for me. I was expected to graduate high school, go to college, and have a great career. The pressure of carrying the hopes and dreams of my family weighed on me. I didn't even know if I still believed I could be and do anything. How could I become when I didn't even know who I was? They thought I did. They didn't know I was hiding. I couldn't tell them that it was too much for me. I couldn't say I was scared. They were depending on me. They'd made so many sacrifices. How could I throw it all away? What if I couldn't do it? What if I disappointed them? What if?

The plan was for me to go to Rutgers and live off campus in Plainfield with my grandmother. Then I decided I wanted to go to Spellman in Atlanta and then to the University of Georgia. The truth is I was scared. I knew I should have started applying to schools in my junior year, but put it off until I was a senior. By then, I realized there was no way we could afford college. I always thought the GI Bill would pay for my education. We found out that Korea was never declared a war, so my father was considered a non-war veteran. In my mind, it was easy to give up now that we didn't have the money. A colleague of Mom's told her about student loans and Pell Grants. However, the deadline to submit financial aid requests for Spellman, University of Georgia, and Rutgers had already passed. I thought, "That's it, I just won't go to college. No more pressure." But my mom and I applied to local colleges and universities, one of which was an exclusive college located in the Back Bay here in Boston. I applied at the very last minute. The day I received the acceptance letter was huge. I can still hear the screams of excitement. My mother bragged to everyone she knew that her daughter was going to college. Their dreams were coming to fruition. As they rejoiced, I was scared.

The excitement ended for me in the fall when I stepped onto the campus. I wasn't prepared for the world I'd entered into. I wasn't used to being the only Black woman. I'd never encountered wealthy white people. They spoke differently and acted differently. For the first time, I was being exposed to what wealth and privilege looked like. They seemed surprised that I could speak properly or that I was actually brilliant. Once again, I wanted to be invisible. This time, I took a different approach. I quickly learned their language and their behavior. No one knew I was from the projects. I never talked about my family or how I grew up. I pretended to know about things I had never heard of. I listened with envy as they talked about European vacations when I had never gone any further than Plainfield, New Jersey. I laughed in all the right places and pretended to like music to which I wasn't accustomed. I made the decision to hide in plain sight. Have you experienced this? Have you ever hidden your brilliance or who you were in order to be accepted? This wasn't new behavior for me. I didn't know until much later in my life that the things I learned growing up in "the P" set me up for this.

The environment at school was difficult. I was treated as if I didn't belong. I recall asking a question in class and being berated by the professor. She yelled, "If you came to class more often, you wouldn't ask that question." After class, I approached her and said I've never missed a class. Her response was "Oh, I made a mistake." At the end of my freshman year, I withdrew from school. I had to go home and tell Mom I quit. When I shared with her what was happening on campus, she told me, "Heidi, you can do it." How could I tell her that I couldn't do it—that I'd failed everyone? That I'd disappointed her and my entire family? I was afraid, but I finally owned up to the truth. I couldn't live up to all of the expectations. She hadn't realized the amount of pressure that I'd carried. Sometimes, I still feel as if there is an expectation of me. There are still times when I fear disappointing my mom and my aunts and dishonoring my grandmother's legacy.

To compensate for leaving school, I became a chronic overachiever. The funny thing is that I didn't leave hiding in plain sight behind. I carried it into my career. If I'm honest, I had no clue who I was. I got a job in finance and loved it. I finally found a place where I could thrive. And thrive I did. Mom taught me to never burn a bridge, and I used her wisdom to develop long-standing relationships. I had the opportunity to attend conferences and rub shoulders with the likes of Ken Chenault, who at the time was the CEO and Chairman of American Express. I became a member of the National Association of Urban Bankers and helped to spearhead the national conference held here in Boston. I was doing big things. My connection with a former manager parlayed into my dream job. I walked in the door as assistant vice president and was quickly promoted to vice president. This girl from "the P" with no college degree was responsible for standing up a line of business in the United States and the United Kingdom. I worked with the sales teams to onboard new clients then managed those relationships. I had an apartment just around the corner from St. Paul's Cathedral in London. I was able to travel to Paris and Amsterdam—the same places years earlier I'd envied my classmates for visiting. I was making my family proud. They were telling everyone they knew about my job and my travels. I sent postcards home and brought back gifts for everyone. I was making their dreams come true. Although I was making their dreams come true, none of mine were coming true. I was still hiding in plain sight. Years of hiding had added layers. No longer was it that no one knew I was from "the P," now they didn't know I wasn't degreed. I didn't talk about the abusive marriage I had endured. I couldn't share with anyone the fear of being found out. What if? I thought of an experience I had had earlier in my career. I was having one of those "I need a change" moments and decided I wanted to move into technology. I received a call back for an interview at a small technology firm that was changing the game. I just knew with my background I would be made an offer. Following what I thought was a successful interview, I met with the recruiter. I didn't know it at the time that what he said would revolutionize my entire life. He said "Heidi, you're the smartest person I've met, and you're comfortable in your own skin" (so he thought.) I was thinking, "Here comes the offer." Then he said, "You need to be degreed. I can't make you an offer at this time." I was stunned. I thought, "Why bring me in just to tell me that?" As I walked out of his office, I had to acknowledge the truth. I had hidden for so long and lived for everyone else for so long that I didn't focus on the need to be degreed. My focus was on being comfortable in my own skin. In that moment, I realized three lessons that I want to leave with you.

1. You don't need to hide in plain sight. The fact that you made it into the room says you're enough. But just being in the room isn't enough. How you show up is what's important. Show up in all your brilliance. You were built differently. How you show up in this moment will determine your next. I forgot the sacrifices the women in my family made so that I could stand in places they never knew existed. My being in the room reintroduced my family to what Black middle-class life looked like.

2. Mindset determines your success and your failure. What you say and believe about who you are and what you want determines what you will receive. James Allen, the author of *As a Man Thinketh*, said "Our souls attract what we secretly harbor, what we love and what we fear." Ask yourself, "What have I manifested in my life?" Is it what you want or believe about who you are? If not, change your mindset, begin to speak, and believe what you want in your life. When the door opens, walk through it even if you have to do it afraid. I learned this about myself. I'm not afraid to fail. I know what failure looks like, and I know how to get up. My fear was "What if I actually can?" In the words of Audre Lorde, "When I dare to be powerful, to use my strength in the service of my

vision, then it becomes less and less important whether I am afraid."

3. Your past doesn't dictate your future. It's a stepping stone. I was ashamed that I grew up in "the P" and that we didn't have a lot of money. I lost focus on the fact that I made it out. You made it out of something or somewhere. Your past is the stepping stone to your future. It has taught you to be resilient and resourceful and what it means to put the work in. It has been the source of your transformation into the woman you are today. Your past is the reason that you're destined. Reach back to a young woman looking at her own circumstance believing it's impossible and show her that like you, she can make it!

I challenge you to sit in a quiet place. After a couple of minutes, begin journaling. Answer the following questions. Give yourself permission to be vulnerable.

1. In what ways have you hidden in plain sight? Explain why you hid your brilliance. How did/does it make you feel?

2. What do you say about yourself and your life? Your beliefs are your blueprint.

3. List those things you believe are holding you back. If it is you, add yourself to this list.

4. Your past is the stepping stone. What makes you special?

Review the lists you have created. Select three items that you're able to control. Write a plan for what you will do differently.

About the Authors

Ayah Harper is an 18-year-old entrepreneur, activist, athlete, and now writer from Revere, Massachusetts. Ayah is the owner and founder of an online BLM clothing line called I Got Ur Black Tees, which she started on Etsy in July of 2020 in response to nationwide social unrest. She has since made over 1500 sales and continues to donate a portion of her monthly proceeds to charitable black organizations such as Black Girls Code and The Innocence Project. She lives with her two proud and loving parents, Jalon and Linwood, and is the middle child between her older (20) and younger (15) brothers, Adam and Amir. She will be attending Tufts University next fall to play basketball and major in computer engineering with hopes of earning both an NCAA championship and a master's degree.

To connect, email Ayah at harperhp53@gmail.com

LaTrelle Natosha Chase was born to be a "TrelleBlazer." Hailing from our nation's capital, Washington, DC, she is the proud daughter of Loretta Reed Pinkney and Victor Pinkney. She attended the historic Tuskegee University in Tuskegee, Alabama and later graduated from Cambridge College in Massachusetts with a Bachelor of Arts in Multidisciplinary Studies. She holds a Master of Education in Curriculum Writing from Fitchburg State University. She is a proud educator in the Boston public schools and a salon owner in Hyde Park, Massachusetts. LaTrelle is the proud wife of Tyrone J. Chase. She is a pastor, master communicator, business strategist, and influencer.

To connect, email LaTrelle at trelleblazers@gmail.com or visit her website at www.allthingstrelleblazer.com

Charmaine L. Arthur is a social justice advocate, speaker, writer, and author. She co-authored her first book entitled *The Power of Prayer: Standing in Authority as You Speak God's Word* in 2018. She was born in Trinidad and Tobago and raised in Boston, Massachusetts. She is a Prophetic Intercessor and the Visionary of Facing Our Journey International Ministries and My Melanin Speaks Power, a program designed for young women of color that focuses on self-love. She is a mother of three and grandmother of four girls. Charmaine has dedicated her career to helping hundreds of young men and women overcome social, emotional, and behavior barriers all within the context of career awareness, career exploration, and self-reflection.

To connect, email Charmaine at
facingourjourney61@gmail.com

Mallory is an avid champion for cultural affirmation and trauma-informed whole-people management and has sixteen years of experience in the nonprofit sector. Her experience includes providing programming oversight in the areas of youth development, workforce development, and volunteerism while partnering with government, education, and private organizations. Mallory currently serves as an executive team member for a pioneering youth homelessness organization in Cambridge, Massachusetts. While working in the nonprofit sector, Mallory developed an interest in corporate social responsibility, having partnered with companies to support youth development initiatives across the state. Mallory holds a bachelor's degree in Sociology and Criminology and Law from Suffolk University, a master's degree in Urban Affairs from Boston University, and a Master of Business Administration with a concentration in Human Resources Management from The University of Scranton. She currently resides in Brockton, Massachusetts with her husband and their children.

To connect, email Mallory at inquire@deitytime.com

Wilma Faye Mathis, MA, M.Div., is an ordained minister and avid Bible scholar. She is the visionary for Mom2Mom Ministry: A Place Where Someone Cares, and serves as vice president of a national women's ministry. Professionally, Wilma is an entrepreneur and a senior project manager in healthcare and a contributing author in *An Artistic Tribute to Harriet Tubman*, *The Commission*, *Finding A Better Way*, *Empowering English Language Learners*, and *God's Masterpiece*. She also finds time to volunteer at homeless shelters for women. Educationally, Wilma is a theology teaching assistant. She holds a Master of Arts and Master of Divinity and is currently pursuing her Doctor of Ministry. Wilma is a grateful mom, loves the Lord, and avails herself to be used for God's glory.

To connect, email Wilma at wilmafaye1@gmail.com

Lady Danika is a committed wife, proud mother and professional educator. In 2016, Lady Danika founded I Made it On Broken Pieces Ministries, a women's ministry on healing the hurts of the past in order to walk in healing and wholeness. Published Author is soon to be added to Danika's life achievement, as she is currently completing the manuscript for her first published work, named after the ministry.

Danika is proud to serve alongside her husband, Pastor John Marshall, in ministry at Mount Calvary Church, a thriving ministry located in Boston, Massachusetts. Together, they are blessed to share Ta'Shayla, Danasia, Trinity, Cameron, Alexa, and John Marshall Jr.

Danika's heart's desire is that her life will serve as testament to others: that God can truly take the broken pieces of our past and work them perfectly for our purpose and His plan.

To connect, email Danika at
dukesdanika157@gmail.com

Dretona T. Maddox, RN, PHN, LCSW, is motivated by hardship. She is a suicide loss survivor and endured homelessness as a teen. She overcame adversity, going on to earn her Bachelor of Science in Nursing from the University of Phoenix and her Master of Social Work from the University of Southern California.

Maddox's challenges were the catalyst for her life's work. She is dedicated to trailblazing as an in-demand public speaker, a Teen Parent Advocate™, and the Founding Executive Director of Purposely Chosen, Inc., a nonprofit organization that provides support and advocacy services to pregnant and parenting teens in foster care. This organization includes two maternity homes in Southern California.

Working for over 27 years as both a nurse and social work practitioner, Dretona balances her love of having an impact in others' lives with that of supporting her six children, her four beautiful grandchildren, and her husband of 29 years, Keith L. Maddox.

Learn more at www.dretonamaddox.com

Heidi Lewis is an ordained elder, a prophetic minister, an internationally acclaimed speaker, and an award-winning and bestselling author. She is the author of *Can I Rest A While?* and a co-author in *Soulful Prayers Volumes 1* and *2* and *Soulful Affirmations*. She has her Bachelor of Science in Management from Boston University and a Master of Business Administration in Organizational Leadership from Norwich University and a Heidi is a member of the Pentimenti Women Writers Group, a mentor with YearUp, a board member for Friends of Young Achievers, and a Diversity Equity and Inclusion Strategist. She lives in Boston, Massachusetts.

Bibliography

"11 Terms You Should Know to Better Understand Structural Racism." Aspen Institute, July 11, 2016. https://www.aspeninstitute.org/blog-posts/structural-racism-definition/.

Allen, J. (2016) "James Allen Complete Collection 21 Books." Palmera Publishing LLC

Audre Lorde Quotes (Author of Sister Outsider) https://www.goodreads.com/author/quotes/18486.Audre_Lorde

Davis, Julia C. and DeFazio, Jeanne C. "An Artistic Tribute to Harriet Tubman." Resource Publications. Eugene: 2021.

Frye, Jocelyn. "Racism and Sexism Combine to Shortchange Working Black Women." 8/22/2019. https://www.americanprogress.org/issues/women/news/2019/08/22/473775/racism-sexism-combine-shortchange-working-black-women/.

Marianne Williamson Quotes (Author of A Return to Love) https://www.goodreads.com/author/quotes/17297.Marianne_Williamson

Wingfield, Adia Harvey. "Women are advancing in the workplace, but women of color are still lagging behind." 10/2020 Brookings Institute. https://www.brookings. edu/essay/women-are-advancing-in-the-workplace- but-women-of-color-still-lag-behind/.

CPSIA information can be obtained
at www.ICGtesting.com
Printed in the USA
LVHW051341021221
704798LV00003B/83